I admire these two men for tackling subje[ct] [...] demands answers. Men and women need g[uiding] principles to help them navigate the treacherous waters of today. This book impacts the personal life of a man relying on the vertical and horizontal aspects of Christian living. Every pastor should have one in his library, and every man should carry one in his back pocket.

DANIEL DE LEON—PRESIDENT, ALIANZA DE MINISTERIOS EVANGELICOS NACIONALES (AMEN)

From the moment we receive the Lord Jesus Christ as our Savior, our eternal destiny is in perspective. Our eternal goal, starting immediately, is to be a worshipper before Almighty God. Tom Fortson and Hank Hanegraaff clearly show us the true North Star.

BISHOP PHILLIP PORTER, CHURCH OF GOD IN CHRIST

Navigating life successfully is not about the questions (we all have a lot of them) it's answers that are important. In this book Tom Fortson and Hank Hanegraaff address the questions that aim us toward the kinds of answers that really count in a man's life. Their aim is good . . . this book is a bulls-eye!

DR. JOSEPH M STOWELL, SR.—AUTHOR, SPEAKER, FORMER PRESIDENT OF MOODY BIBLE INSTITUTE

Brief is better! Tom Fortson and Hank Hanegraaff have skillfully and artfully blended two short but powerful books into Seven Questions of a Promise Keeper. *The first book (chapters 1-3, 7) establishes solid foundations in scripture, and the second book (chapters 4-6) grounds us in vital men's issues.*

SAMUEL L. WINDER—PROMISE KEEPERS BOARD MEMBER, NAVAJO/SOUTHERN UTE INDIAN TRIBE

Fortson and Hanegraaff have captured my attention. They asked me the right question that gave me pause in an overly busy life. That hesitation was then filled with a series of questions that followed an intriguing sequence. If you have felt stuck in life, fearful that you were headed toward a mediocre subsistence, or wondered if your endless activities really made a noticeable difference in the lives of others, or secretly begged God to scratch your unreachable itch for personal significance, then you will want to read this book. It will put you in a conversation of great discovery through great questions. Then you will be well on your way to a deeply satisfying and significant life as a man determined to keep his promises and to enjoy the subsequent fruit that God gives.

BRUCE W. FONG, PH.D—PRESIDENT, MICHIGAN THEOLOGICAL SEMINARY

My dear friend Tom Fortson has written an extremely important book. It is the right message at the right time. Significance, every man needs it. Without it he lacks what he needs to pass on the the next generation. As I have had the privilege to speak many times at a P.K. men's conference, I have emphasized the need to live a legacy. This book gives a road map from survival to significance. Every man needs it!

DR. CRAWFORD W. LORITTS, JR.—AUTHOR, PASTOR, SPEAKER, RADIO HOST

7 QUESTIONS OF A PROMISE KEEPER

Tom Fortson & Hank Hanegraaff
President of Promise Keepers   President of Christian Research Institute (CRI)
and Host of the *Bible Answer Man* broadcast

A Division of Thomas Nelson Publishers
Since 1798
www.thomasnelson.com

Table of Contents

INTRODUCTION

The Seven Questions

It was a beautiful day on the Monterey Peninsula. And I was playing golf with Tom Fortson, the president of Promise Keepers. My mind was focused on shooting the lowest round possible. His mind was focused elsewhere.

I can still vividly remember the scene. I was standing in the middle of the seventh fairway zeroed in on my target with laser-like focus. Before I could pull the trigger Tom broke my concentration. His exact words are still etched in my mind—*"What are the questions every Promise Keeper must be equipped to answer?"*

Although I was one under par at the time, my mind never returned to golf. Tom's vision was far too intoxicating. Simple, yet profound! I instinctively knew that God was at work. And I can still remember precisely how Tom summed up the vision: *"It isn't as important to have all the answers, as it is to be able to identify the right questions."*

My experience in hosting the *Bible Answer Man* broadcast has convinced me that while it is critical to identify the *right questions*, it is also crucial to ask the right questions in the *right sequence*. For example, there is little sense in asking questions regarding biblical ethics prior to answering the question of biblical authority. Likewise, the question, "What would Jesus do?" is trumped by the question, "Who is Jesus?"

Tom's vision is truly a big idea! Equipping Promise Keepers men to ask the right questions could ultimately determine not only the destinies of their children and wives but also the direction of civilization and the world. Take, for example, the abortion debate. The right questions should have been, "What is life?" and "When does

> "It isn't as important to have all the answers, as it is to be able to identify the right questions."
>
> TOM FORTSON

it begin?" Instead the question of "choice" was deemed preeminent. As a result our society is headed into a bioethical holocaust of mythic proportions. Again, the only way to advance in the right direction is to ask the right questions and to ask them in the right sequence.

That day on the Monterey Peninsula I could not help but

draw an ironic comparison between Tom's vision and the way he golfed his ball. No matter how far he hit his drives they always seemed headed in the wrong direction. The results were often catastrophic! In the things that mattered, however, Tom was headed straight for the target. By the time we reached the clubhouse we had settled on seven significant questions that every Promise Keeper must be equipped to ask and answer. And that night, before my head hit the pillow, I had organized them around the acronym *P-R-O-M-I-S-E*.

In order of priority, three major questions regarding worldview must be asked and answered. The first involves the planet we call home: "Is Earth a *Privileged planet* created by a personal uncaused First Cause (an eternal God) or is it merely a function of random processes?" In the final analysis, more consequences for society hinge on this issue than on any other. Chief among them are the preservation of meaning, morality, and mission. In the end, how a Promise Keeper views his origin will determine how he lives his life.

Next in sequence is the question of resurrection: "Did Jesus Christ rise from the dead, thus demonstrating that He is God, or is *Resurrection* mere wishful thinking?" The apostle Paul put it plainly, *"And if Christ has not been raised, our preaching is useless and so is your faith"* (1 Corinthians 15:14). In other words, the whole of Christianity hinges on the reality of resurrection. If Christ has not been raised, *"we are to be pitied more than all men"* (1 Corinthians 15:19). If Christ has been raised, we are guaranteed eternity.

Third in order of priority, I address the origin of the Scripture. "Is the *Origin of the Bible* divine or is it merely human in origin?" If the Bible is merely human in origin, then it stands in a long line of peers with other holy books. If, however, we can demonstrate the Old and New Testaments to be divine in origin, they are the authority by which to govern our lives. Without the enduring reference point of Scriptural authority, societal norms are reduced to mere matters of preference.

The second series of questions in sequence pertain to men as relational beings. The first question in this series involves the foundational building block of society—the family: "What makes *Men* so strategic to the proper ordering of a society?" Without recognizing their God-ordained responsibilities to lead their families, Promise Keepers men will ultimately miss the broader purposes of God in the culture at large.

Next is the issue of isolationism, which is a significant obstacle for men in fulfilling their God-ordained responsibilities. Thus the pressing question: "How does the Promise Keepers movement address the danger of *Isolationism?*" Isolationism and lack of accountability is not only dangerous to our spiritual well-being, it is damaging to our society. Addressing this question head-on will ultimately serve as an antidote to pandemics ranging from infidelity to pornography.

The last of the three relational questions involves significance: "How can I progress from *survival to Significance?*" Most men trudge through life merely seeking to survive. Jesus, however, came to give us an unsurpassed quality of life. In the words of the Master: *"I have come that they may have life and may have it more abundantly"* (John 10:10). God has given every Promise Keeper time, talent, and treasure to be used for His glory and for the extension of His kingdom. There is no greater enterprise! There is no greater calling! In the pithy words of C. S. Lewis: "Enemy-occupied territory—that is what this world is. Christianity is the story of how the rightful king has landed, you might say landed in disguise, and is calling us all to take part in a great campaign of sabotage."[1]

The seventh and final question involves perspective. "Why is it so crucial for Promise Keepers men to develop an *Eternal*

Equipping a generation of Promise Keepers to ask the right questions and to ask them in the right sequence may well become a catalyst for changing the very course of civilization.

perspective?" No one has answered this question more eloquently than the apostle Paul. Pressing the analogy of athletics, he writes, *"Do you not know that in a race all the runners run, but only one gets the prize? Run in such a way as to get the prize. Everyone who competes in the games goes into strict training.*

They do it to get a crown that will not last; but we do it to get a crown that will last forever" (1 Corinthians 9:24-25). Thus says Paul, *"I do not run like a man running aimlessly; I do not fight like a man beating the air. No, I beat my body and make it my slave so that after I have preached to others, I myself will not be disqualified for the prize"* (vv. 26-27).

In the end, equipping a generation of Promise Keepers to ask the right questions and to ask them in the right sequence may well become a catalyst for changing the very course of civilization. But change begins at home. To paraphrase the immortal words of President John F. Kennedy, "Ask not what your family can do for you. Ask what you can do for your family." If you do, God will use you to both strengthen the family of God and bring salvation to the family of man. Tom and I have a dream. Come share it with us.

QUESTION 1

Is Earth a Privileged Planet Created by a Personal Uncaused First Cause or Is It Merely a Function of Random Processes?

HOW A PROMISE KEEPER VIEWS HIS ORIGINS WILL ULTIMATELY DETERMINE HOW HE LIVES HIS LIFE

"The cosmos is all that is, or ever was, or ever will be."

CARL SAGAN

"In the beginning God created the heavens and the earth."

THE PROPHET MOSES (GENESIS 1:1)

The question of origins is not just *an* apologetic question. It is *the* apologetic question. How one views his origins will inevitably determine how he lives his life. If a man believes that he is a function of random chance, he will live his life by a different standard than if he knows that he is created in the image of God and accountable to God. That, of course, begs the question: Is Earth a Privileged planet created by a personal uncaused first cause or is it merely a function of chance processes? The answer to this question forms the foundation for every other aspect of our worldview. If the Creator is, chance is not; if chance is, the Creator is not.

THE SITUATION

It is not uncommon for Christians to be accused of relying on superstition and unscientific supernaturalism because of our belief that the earth on which we reside is a privileged planet. Such accusations emanate from the ivy-covered walls of prestigious Western universities, to the aisles of the local Wal-Marts, to water coolers in the workplace. Though the opponents of Intelligent Design claim to view the world through an unbiased, objective, and purely scientific lens, their approach to science is at its core an expression of an ideology known as *philosophical naturalism*.

Philosophical naturalism can be defined as "the view that the space-time material universe is all there is."[2] Accordingly, the existence of God and the possibility of miracles are ruled out on the basis of philosophical prejudices before any exploration of the natural world even gets off the ground. As philosopher of science, William Dembski observes:

> *Naturalism is in the air we breathe. It pervades our cultural atmosphere. We see it whenever the mysteries of the faith are ridiculed. We see it whenever a PBS nature program credits nature for some object of wonder instead of God. We see it whenever psychologists claim to have gotten to the root of our problems but forget that we are fallen beings made in God's image. We see it, alas, whenever we forget God and worship the creature more than the Creator.*[3]

Dembski goes on to point out that, "Within Western culture, naturalism has become the default position for all serious inquiry. From biblical studies to law to education to science to the arts, inquiry is allowed to proceed only under the supposition that nature is self-contained."[4]

Thus, far from practicing open-minded science, naturalists close their minds to supernatural explanations for the origin of our planet.

To their way of thinking there are only two possible answers to the question, "Where on Earth did earth come from?" The first is that the Earth, along with the rest of this time-space universe, ultimately sprang into existence out of nothing. And the second is that the universe eternally existed. Such prejudices are remarkably easy to dismiss.

To begin with, the notion that our universe sprang into existence out of nothing flies in the face of plain old common sense. It doesn't take a rocket scientist to understand that an effect must have a cause equal to or greater than itself. As Julie Andrews sings it in the *Sound of Music*, "Nothing comes from nothing; nothing ever could."

Furthermore, like the law of cause and effect, the law of energy conservation is an empirical law of science. Also known as the First Law of Thermodynamics, the Law of Conservation of Energy states that while energy *can* be converted from one form to another, the natural universe in and of itself *cannot* create or annihilate anything. Thus it is not only logically impossible but scientifically implausible to suppose that our universe sprang into existence out of nothing by nothing.

Finally, in saying that the universe is an effect that requires a cause greater than itself, one might presume that this principle would apply equally to God. This, however, is clearly not the case. Unlike the universe, which according to modern science had a beginning, God is eternal. Thus, as an eternal being, God is the uncaused First Cause.

While the Law of Conservation of Energy is a blow to naturalism, the Law of Entropy is a bullet to its head. As such, it is the death knell to the second naturalistic explanation—namely, that the universe eternally existed. The universe is dying of heat loss because, according to the law of entropy, also known as the second law of thermodynamics, heat flows spontaneously from hot to cold.

While we should fight for a person's right to have faith in science fiction, we must resist the evolutionary attempt to brainwash people into thinking that naturalism is good science.

In other words, everything ultimately runs from order to disorder and from complexity to decay. The sun burns up billions of tons of hydrogen each second, stars burn out, and species eventually become extinct. If the universe were eternal, then, it would have died of heat loss an eternity ago. Thus, proponents of naturalism would do well to heed the words of the mathematician and physicist Sir Arthur Eddington:

"If your theory is found to be against the second law of thermo-dynamics, I can give you no hope; there is nothing for it but to collapse in deepest humiliation."[5]

While we should fight for a person's right to have faith in science fiction, we must resist the evolutionary attempt to brainwash people into thinking that naturalism is good science.

THE STAKES

Other than Scripture, Darwin's magnum opus, *The Origin of Species*, might well be the most significant literary work in the annals of recorded history. Sir Julian Huxley called the evolutionary dogma it spawned "the most powerful and the most comprehensive idea that has ever arisen on earth."[6]

The far-reaching consequences of this cosmogenic myth can be felt in every academic enterprise as well as every echelon of education. The most significant consequence, however, is that it undermines the very foundation of Christianity. If indeed evolution is reflective of the laws of science, Genesis must be reflective of the flaws of Scripture. And if the foundation of Christianity is flawed, the superstructure is destined to fall.

While the evolutionary system is thought to be cutting edge, in reality it is the mere repackaging of an age-old deception. In the very first book of the Bible, Satan tells Eve that if she eats the forbidden fruit, her eyes will be opened and she will be like God, knowing good and evil (Genesis 3:5). Put another way, Eve would become the final court of arbitration—she would determine what was right and what was wrong.

In the nineteenth century, this repackaging of Satan's age-old deception manifested in Darwin's notion of the survival of the fittest in the struggle for life. Consider the following excerpt from a letter written by Charles Darwin in 1881: "The more civilized so-called Caucasian races have beaten the Turkish hollow in the struggle for existence. Looking to the world at no very distant date, what an endless number of the lower races will have been eliminated by the higher civilized races throughout the world."[7] Darwin repeated this sentiment in his book, *The Descent of Man*. He speculated, "At some future period, not very distant as measured by centuries, the civilized races of man will almost certainly exterminate and replace the savage races throughout the world."[8] In addition, he subtitled his magnum opus, *The*

Preservation of Favored Races in the Struggle for Life.[9]

And Darwin was not alone in his racist ideology. Thomas Huxley, who coined the term "agnostic"[10] and was the man most responsible for advancing Darwinian doctrine, argued that "no rational man, cognizant of the facts, believes that the average negro is the *equal, still less the superior,* of the white man. . . . It is simply incredible that . . . he will be able to compete successfully with his *bigger-brained and smaller-jawed rival,* in a contest which is to be carried on by *thoughts* and not by *bites.*"[11]

In sharp distinction, biblical Christianity makes it crystal clear that in Christ *"there is neither Jew nor Greek, slave nor free, male nor female"* (Galatians 3:28).[12] It is significant to note that Crusaders who used force to further their creeds in the name of God were acting in direct opposition to the teachings of Christ. Conversely, the teachings of Huxley and others like him are completely consistent with the teachings of Darwin. Indeed, social Darwinism has provided the scientific substructure for some of the most significant atrocities in human history.

Adolf Hitler's philosophy that Jews were subhuman and that Aryans were supermen led to the extermination of six million

Jews. In the words of Sir Arthur Keith, a militant anti-Christian physical anthropologist: "The German Fuhrer, as I have consistently maintained, is an evolutionist; he has consistently sought to make the practices of Germany conform to the theory of evolution."[13]

Karl Marx, the father of Communism, saw in Darwinism the scientific and sociological support for an economic experiment that eclipsed even the carnage of Hitler's Germany. His hatred of Christ and Christianity led to the mass murder of multiplied millions worldwide. Karl Marx so revered Darwin that his desire was to dedicate a portion of *Das Kapital* to him.[14]

Sigmund Freud, the founder of modern psychology, was also a faithful follower of Charles Darwin. His belief that man was merely a sophisticated animal led him to postulate that "anxiety, paranoia and other mental disorders each embody modes of behavior that were once adaptive for the human species in the stages of evolution."[15]

Yet all of this is but the tip of an insidious iceberg. If our planet is merely a function of blind naturalistic processes, there is no ultimate *meaning* to life, no foundation for *morality,* and no transcendent *mission* for living lives that count for time and for eternity.

MEANING

First, in a world that comes into being through the accidental convergence of natural processes, human existence is rendered meaningless. The universe will ultimately pass out of existence, the human race with it, and it matters not whether either had ever existed at all. As philosopher William Lane Craig has observed, philosophical naturalism carried to its logical conclusion paints a picture of a world in which "mankind is a doomed race in a dying universe. Because the human race will eventually cease to exist, it makes no ultimate difference whether it ever did exist."[16] Indeed, in such a world, "mankind is thus no more significant than a swarm of mosquitoes or a barnyard of pigs, for their end is all the same. The same blind cosmic process that coughed them up in the first place will eventually swallow them all again."[17]

Such philosophers as Albert Camus and Friedrich Nietzsche realized this and ended up adopting a hopeless view of the world in which it makes no difference whether one is alive or dead. Camus concluded his novel *The Stranger* with the protagonist finally coming to grips with the "benign indifference of the universe," and as he faced execution for murder he concluded that "all that remained to hope was that on the day of my execution there should be a huge crowd of spectators and that they should greet me with howls of execration."[18]

A world without God is a world emptied of hope, meaning, and significance. Thus, when confronted by those who adhere to the "enlightened" philosophy of naturalism we must follow the lead of philosopher James Sire by asking, "Could a being thrown up by chance be worthy?"[19]

MORALITY

Furthermore, in a world without God, all life ultimately proceeds from matter alone. Thus, death is nothing more than the beginning of a process by which the molecules that make up our bodies are redistributed into the vast impersonal cosmos. In a purely naturalistic universe there can be no existence after death, and in a world without God there can be no ultimate judgment for immoral behavior or reward for righteousness.

Craig writes, "If life ends at the grave, then it makes no difference whether one has lived as a Stalin or as a saint."[20] Indeed, in the absence of a transcendent heavenly Judge, the wrongs of

Hitler's holocaust will never be righted. After slaughtering six million Jews, Hitler merely died in the comforting arms of his mistress with no eternal consequences. In such a world there can be no genuine justice.

Morality may be summed up as the obligations we have to behave rightly toward one another and toward God. Obviously, in a world without God, morality cannot be said to include any obligation to act rightly toward Him. Likewise, in a world without God there is no ultimate objective ground for the moral treatment of God's creation. Without a transcendent moral lawgiver there cannot be a universal moral law. In the absence of an objective standard of right and wrong, we are left without a basis for criticisms of such horrendous evils as racism, genocide, and rape, let alone lesser violations of moral behavior. In a purely naturalistic world, "moral values are either just expressions of personal taste or the by-products of socio-biological evolution and conditioning."[21]

Indeed, in a world without God, sexual promiscuity, racism, and murder become morally indistinguishable from love, equality and justice.

MISSION

Finally, common wisdom says, "You can't know where you're going if you don't know where you're from." Though this remark is usually made in superficial contexts, the truth is that in the absence of a relationship with your Maker, you will never be able to discover your mission. If we are the result of blind naturalistic processes, there is ultimately no purpose to life. There is no transcendent mission. No end for which to strive. No destiny. Only death awaits.

> In the absence of God there is no meaning to ground the value of our existence, no firm foundation for moral living, and no mission toward which to direct our lives.

In the absence of God there is no meaning to ground the value of our existence, no firm foundation for moral living, and no mission toward which to direct our lives. All that is left is to despair. To live in such a world requires that one pretend that life is meaningful without God, but at the end of the day that is nothing more than wishful make-believe.

THE SOLUTION

It is one thing to curse the darkness. It is quite another to build a lighthouse in the midst of a gathering storm. As previously noted,

Promise Keepers men should be equipped to demonstrate that naturalistic explanations cannot account for the existence of the universe. Only a supernatural explanation can suffice. King David said it best: *"The heavens declare the glory of God; the skies proclaim the work of his hands. Day after day they pour forth speech; night after night they display knowledge. There is no speech or language where their voice is not heard. Their voice goes out into all the earth, their words to the ends of the world"* (Psalm 19:1-4).

As such, we must be ready to demonstrate that our Earth is indeed a *Privileged Planet*. Consider plain old tap water. The solid state of most substances is more dense than their liquid state, but the opposite is true for water, which explains why ice floats rather than sinks. If water were like virtually any other liquid, it would freeze from the bottom up rather than from the top down, killing aquatic life, destroying the oxygen supply, and making Earth uninhabitable.[22] Or consider ocean tides, which are caused by the gravitational pull of the moon and play a crucial role in our survival. If the moon were significantly larger, thereby having a stronger gravitational pull, devastating tidal waves would submerge large areas of land. If the moon were smaller, tidal motion would cease, and the oceans would stagnate and die.[23]

Finally, consider the ideal temperatures on planet Earth—not duplicated on any other known planet in the universe. If we were closer to the sun, we would fry. If we were farther away, we would freeze.[24] As noted by astrobiologist Guillermo Gonzales and philosophical theologian Jay Richards, "our planet is exquisitely fit not only to support life, but also to give us the best view of the universe, as if Earth were designed both for life and scientific discovery."[25]

From tap water to the tides and temperatures that we so easily take for granted, the Earth is an unparalleled planetary masterpiece. Like Handel's *Messiah* or da Vinci's *Last Supper*, it should never be carelessly pawned off as the result of blind naturalistic processes.

> The Promise Keeper recognizes that all life is inherently meaningful; that the foundation for moral living is the Word of God; and that lives lived to the glory of God have a mission.

Naturalism today is in much the same condition as Marxism was before its collapse. Its terminal condition cannot be successfully treated with medieval medications. As the Soviet Union collapsed before our very eyes, so, too, the propped up corpse of philosophical naturalism is ready for its final fall. While insiders are aware of naturalism's desperate condition, the general public is still in the dark.

That's precisely where the Promise Keepers movement can have a dramatic impact. You and I have the inestimable privilege to share the news that nothing could be more compelling in an age of scientific enlightenment than: *"In the beginning God created the heavens and the earth"* (Genesis 1:1). According to this supremely rational and scientifically viable view of creation, the Promise Keeper recognizes that all life is inherently meaningful; that the foundation for moral living is the Word of God; and that lives lived to the glory of God have a mission. A mission aptly codified in the Seven Promises of a Promise Keeper:

1. A Promise Keeper is committed to honoring Jesus Christ through worship, prayer and obedience to God's Word in the power of the Holy Spirit.

2. A Promise Keeper is committed to pursuing vital relationships with a few other men, understanding that he needs brothers to help him keep his promises.

3. A Promise Keeper is committed to practicing spiritual, moral, ethical, and sexual purity.

4. A Promise Keeper is committed to building strong marriages and families through love, protection and biblical values.

5. A Promise Keeper is committed to supporting the mission of his church by honoring and praying for his pastor, and by actively giving his time and resources.

6. A Promise Keeper is committed to reaching beyond any racial and denominational barriers to demonstrate the power of biblical unity.

7. A Promise Keeper is committed to influencing his world, being obedient to the Great Commandment (see Mark 12:30-31) and the Great Commission (see Matthew 28:19-20).

QUESTION 2

Is the Resurrection Mere Wishful Thinking Or Did Jesus Christ Rise From the Dead, Thus Demonstrating That He is God?

IF JESUS WAS NOT RESURRECTED, PROMISE KEEPERS MIGHT JUST AS WELL EAT, DRINK, AND BE MERRY FOR TOMORROW WE DIE

"The tales of entombment and resurrection were latter-day wishful thinking. Instead, Jesus' corpse went the way of all abandoned criminals' bodies: it was probably barely covered with dirt, vulnerable to the wild dogs that roamed the wasteland of the execution grounds."

JOHN DOMINIC CROSSAN, COFOUNDER OF THE JESUS SEMINAR

"If there is no resurrection of the dead, then not even Christ has been raised. And if Christ has not been raised, our preaching is useless and so is your faith."

THE APOSTLE PAUL (1 CORINTHIANS 15:13-14)

If liberal scholars, adherents of world religions, or devotees of the kingdom of the cults are correct, the resurrection of Christ is fiction, fantasy, or fraud. If, on the other hand, Christianity is factually reliable, the resurrection of Jesus Christ is the greatest feat in human history. No middle ground exists. The resurrection is history or hoax, miracle or myth, fact or fantasy.

THE SITUATION

As I write this chapter, Dan Brown's fictional phenomenon, *The Da Vinci Code*,[26] is enjoying its 154th week on *The New York Times* Best Seller list. Brown's novel has now sold over 40 million copies and shows no signs of waning in popularity. A Sony Pictures movie release starring Oscar winning actor Tom Hanks and directed by Oscar winner Ron Howard will no doubt continue to give the book long legs.

> The resurrection is history or hoax, miracle or myth, fact or fantasy.

If there was ever a clear example of popularity not being a test for truth, *The Da Vinci Code* is it. *The Da Vinci Code* not only perpetuates the myth that Jesus was married and the notion that Christianity was concocted to subjugate women, but it also undermines the resurrection of Jesus Christ.[27] In the world of *The Da Vinci Code*, one would naturally assume that Christ's resurrection is mere mythology borrowed from the ancient pagan mystery religions.

Though communicated through the medium of fiction, Brown's historically revisionist claims are intended to be understood as fact. Indeed, *Library Journal* characterized *The Da Vinci Code* as "a compelling blend of history and page-turning suspense," a "masterpiece" that "should be mandatory reading."[28] *Publisher's Weekly* called it "an exhaustively researched page-turner about secret religious societies, ancient cover-ups and savage vengeance."[29] Brown himself says he is so confident in the reliability of his claims that were he to write a nonfiction piece on the same theme, he would not change a thing.[30]

While *The Da Vinci Code* is currently the most popular attack on the deity of Jesus and His resurrection from the dead, it is by no means unique. Since the advent of "higher criticism" it has become increasingly popular for liberal scholars to deny the historicity of the resurrection, suggesting instead that "tales of entombment and resurrection" were latter-day wishful thinking. Likwise, world religions such as Islam contend that Jesus was never crucified and, thus, never resurrected. In Muslim lore, God made someone appear to be Jesus, and the look-a-like was thus crucified in His place. Yet other attacks emanate from the kingdom of the cults. Jehovah's Witnesses for example claim that Jesus was not resurrected but rather recreated by God as an immaterial spirit creature.[31]

THE STAKES

As Paul makes clear in his first letter to the Corinthian Christians, the stakes in the debate concerning resurrection could not be higher.

> *And if Christ has not been raised, your faith is futile; you are still in your sins. Then those also who have fallen asleep in Christ are lost. If only for this life we have hope in Christ, we are to be pitied more than all men. (1 Corinthians 15:17-19)*

No middle ground exists. The resurrection is either the greatest fiction in the annals of recorded history or it is its greatest feat. As such, it follows directly on the heels of origins as the most significant apologetic issue. The God who created the universe is not merely transcendent, He has condescended to cloak Himself in human flesh, He has come to live among us, and He has demonstrated that He is indeed God through the immutable fact of His resurrection.

If Christ's death for the atonement of sin was not vindicated through His resurrection, then we have no hope of being resurrected ourselves. In fact, as Paul put it, *"If the dead are not raised, 'Let us eat and drink, for tomorrow we die'"* (1 Corinthians 15:32). In truth, the resurrection is not merely important to the historic Christian faith, without it, there would be no Christianity. It is the singular doctrine that elevates Christianity above all other world religions. Through the resurrection, Christ demonstrated that He does not stand in a line of peers with Abraham, Buddha, or Confucius. He is utterly unique. He has the power not only to lay down His life, but the power to take it up again.

> Through the Resurrection, Christ demonstrated that He does not stand in a line of peers with Abraham, Buddha, or Confucius. He is utterly unique. He has the power not only to lay down His life, but the power to take it up again.

It is precisely because of the strategic significance of the resurrection that Promise Keepers men must be prepared to defend its historicity. Thus, apologetics—the defense of the faith—has a dual purpose. On the one hand, apologetics involves pre-evangelism. In post-Christian America, few people are aware that belief in the resurrection is not a blind leap into the dark, but rather faith founded on fact. It is historic and evidential. Thus, it is defensible. On the other hand, apologetics involves post-evangelism. In an age in which the resurrection is under siege by books such as *The Da Vinci Code*, knowing how to defend its reliability serves to strengthen our faith.

THE SOLUTION

Because of its centrality to Christianity, I've developed the acronym F-E-A-T as an enduring reminder that, far from being a gargantuan fraud, the resurrection is the greatest feat in the annals of recorded history. Each letter will remind you of an undeniable fact of the resurrection.

FATAL TORMENT

The fatal torment of Christ as recounted in the New Testament is one of the most well-established facts of ancient history. In our age of scientific enlightenment, there is now virtual consensus among New Testament scholars, both conservative and liberal, that Jesus died on the cross, that He was buried in the tomb of Joseph of Arimathea, and that His death drove His disciples to despair.[32]

The best medical minds of ancient and modern times have demonstrated beyond a shadow of a doubt that Christ's physical trauma was fatal.[33] His torment began in the Garden of Gethsemane after an emotional Last Supper. There Jesus experienced a medical condition known as hematidrosis. Tiny capillaries in His sweat glands ruptured, mixing sweat with blood.

Before Caiaphas the high priest, He was mocked, beaten, and spat upon. The next morning, Jesus, battered, bruised, and bleeding, was led into the Praetorium. There He was stripped and subjected to the brutality of Roman flogging. A whip replete with razor-sharp bones and lead balls reduced His body to quivering ribbons of bleeding flesh. As Christ slumped into the pool of His own blood, the soldiers threw a scarlet robe across His shoulders, thrust a scepter into His hands, and pressed sharp thorns into His scalp.

After they mocked Him, they took the scepter out of His hands and repeatedly struck Him on the head. By now, Jesus was in critical condition. A heavy wooden beam was thrust upon Christ's bleeding body, and He was led away to a place called Golgotha. There the Lord experienced ultimate physical torture in the form of the cross.

At "the place of the skull," Roman soldiers drove thick, seven-inch iron spikes through Christ's hands[34] and feet. In the ensuing hours, He experienced cycles of joint-wrenching cramps, intermittent asphyxiation, and excruciating pain as His lacerated back scraped up and down against the rough timber of the cross.

Shortly thereafter, a Roman legionnaire drove his spear through the fifth interspace between the ribs, upward through the pericardium, and into Christ's heart. From the wound rushed forth blood and water, demonstrating conclusively that Jesus had suffered fatal torment.

In light of all the evidence, believing that Jesus merely swooned must surely stretch credulity beyond the breaking point. It would mean that Christ survived six trials, a lack of sleep, the scourge, being spiked to a cross, and a spear wound in His side. Then He survived three days without medical attention, single-handedly rolled away an enormously heavy tombstone, subdued an armed guard, strolled around on pierced feet, seduced His disciples into lying that He had conquered death, and then lived out the remainder of His life in obscurity. If one can believe that myth, it should be no problem whatsoever to believe in the miracle of resurrection. No wonder, then, that critics of the New Testament have argued that the swoon hypothesis just described is not viable.[35]

EMPTY TOMB

As the reliability of the resurrection is undermined in books such as *The Da Vinci Code*, it is crucial that Promise Keepers are prepared to demonstrate that Jesus was buried and that on Easter morning some two thousand years ago, the tomb was empty. Contrary to John Dominic Crossan's dogmatic assertion that Jesus' body was likely eaten by wild dogs that roamed the execution grounds,[36] the liberal Cambridge scholar John A. T. Robinson conceded that the burial of Christ "is one of the earliest and best-attested facts about Jesus."[37] This statement is not merely a dogmatic assertion, but rather stands firmly upon sound argumentation.

As in the case of fatal torment, liberal and conservative scholars alike agree that the body of Jesus was buried in the private tomb of Joseph of Arimathea. William Lane Craig underscores this fact in his public debate with John Dominic Crossan by noting that, as a member of the Jewish court that condemned Jesus to death, Joseph of Arimathea is unlikely to be Christian fiction.[38] Additionally, Craig notes that no competing burial story exists and the fact that the account of Jesus' burial in the tomb of Joseph of Arimathea is substantiated by Mark's Gospel dates the story far too early to have been the subject of legendary corruption.[39]

Furthermore, as Craig explains during his interview with Lee Strobel in *The Case for Christ*, "when you understand the role of women in first-century Jewish society, what's really extraordinary is that this empty tomb story should feature females as the discoverers of the empty tomb." In fact, "any later legendary account would have certainly portrayed male disciples as discovering the tomb—Peter or John, for example. The fact that women are the first witnesses to the empty tomb is most plausibly explained by the reality that—like it or not—they were the discoverers of the empty tomb! This shows that the gospel writers faithfully recorded what happened, even if it was embarrassing."[40]

Finally, as Craig explains in *Jesus Under Fire*, the earliest Jewish response to the resurrection of Jesus Christ presupposes the empty tomb. Instead of denying that the tomb was empty, the antagonists of Christ accused His disciples of stealing the body. Their response to the proclamation "He is risen—He is risen indeed!" was not "His body is still in the tomb," or "He was thrown into a shallow grave and eaten by dogs." Instead, they responded, *"His disciples came during the night and stole him away"* (Matthew 28:13).[41] In the centuries following the resurrection, the fact of the empty tomb was forwarded by Jesus' friends and foes alike.

APPEARANCES OF CHRIST

In the Acts of the Apostles, Dr. Luke writes that Jesus gave the disciples *"many convincing proofs that he was alive. He appeared to them over a period of forty days and spoke about the kingdom of God"* (Acts 1:3). Likewise, Peter in his powerful Pentecost proclamation confidently communicated that many credible eyewitnesses could confirm the fact of Christ's physical post-resurrection appearances (Acts 2:29-32). Like the apostle Peter, the apostle Paul exudes confidence in the appearances of Christ. In his first letter to the Corinthian Christians, he provides the following details and descriptions:

> *For what I received I passed on to you as of first importance: that Christ died for our sins according to the Scriptures, that he was buried, that he was raised on the third day according to the Scriptures, and that he appeared to Peter, and then to the Twelve. After that, he appeared to more than five hundred of the brothers at the same time, most of whom are still living, though some have fallen asleep. Then he appeared to James, then to all the apostles, and last of all he appeared to me also, as to one abnormally born.* (1 Corinthians 15:3-8)

One thing can be stated with iron-clad certainty: The apostles did not merely propagate Christ's teachings; they were absolutely positive that He had appeared to them in the flesh. Although we are now two thousand years removed from the actual event, we, too, can be absolutely confident in Christ's post-resurrection appearances.

One of the principal reasons for this confidence is that within the passage cited above (1 Corinthians 15:3-8) Paul is reiterating a Christian creed that can be traced all the way back to the formative stages of the early Christian church.[42] Incredibly, scholars of all stripes agree that this creed can be dated to within three to eight years of the crucifixion itself.[43] The short time span between Christ's crucifixion and the composition of this early Christian creed precludes the possibility of legendary corruption.[44]

Not only so, but Peter, Paul, and the rest of the apostles claimed that Christ appeared to hundreds of people who were still alive and available for cross-examination.[45] As quoted above, Paul claims that Christ *"appeared to more than five hundred of the brothers at the same time, most of whom are still living, though some have fallen asleep"* (1 Corinthians 15:6). It would have been one thing to attribute these supernatural experiences to people who had already died. It was quite another to attribute them to multitudes who were still alive.

As the famed New Testament scholar of Cambridge University C. H. Dodd points out, "There can hardly be any purpose in mentioning the fact that most of the five hundred are still alive, unless Paul is saying, in effect, 'The witnesses are there to be questioned.'"[46] Says Craig, "Paul could never have said this if the event had not occurred; he could not have challenged people to ask the witnesses if the event had not taken place and there were no witnesses. But evidently there were witnesses to this event. . . . Therefore, the event must have taken place."[47]

No one summed up the consensus of both liberal and conservative scholarship better than New Testament scholar Norman Perrin: "The more we study the tradition with regard to the appearances, the firmer the rock begins to appear upon which they are based."[48]

TRANSFORMATION

What happened as a result of the resurrection is unprecedented in human history. In the span of a few hundred years, a small band of seemingly insignificant believers succeeded in turning an entire empire upside down. While it is conceivable that the disciples would have faced torture, vilification, and even cruel deaths for what they fervently believed to be true, it is inconceivable that they would have been willing to die for what they knew to be a lie. As Dr. Simon Greenleaf, the famous Royall Professor of Law at Harvard put it: "If it were morally possible for them to have been deceived in this matter, every human motive operated to lead them to discover and avow their error. To have persisted in so gross a falsehood, after it was known to them, was not only to encounter, for life, all the evils which man could inflict from without, but to endure also the pangs of inward and conscious guilt; with no hope of future peace, no testimony of a good conscience, no expectation of honor or esteem among men, no hope of happiness in this life, or in the world to come. . . . If then their testimony was not true, there was no possible motive for this fabrication."[49]

As Greenleaf so masterfully communicates, the Twelve[50] were thoroughly transformed by the resurrection. Peter, who was once afraid of a young woman exposing him as a follower of Christ, after the resurrection was transformed into a lion of the faith and suffered a martyr's death.[51] According to tradition, he requested to be crucified upside down, because he felt unworthy to be crucified in the same manner as his Lord.[52]

James, the half-brother of Jesus, who once opposed his brother (John 7:5), after the resurrection calls himself *"a bond-servant . . . of the Lord Jesus Christ"* (James 1:1). He not only became the leader of the Jerusalem church, but in about A.D. 62 was martyred for his faith.[53] Eusebius of Caesarea describes how James was thrown from the pinnacle of the temple and subsequently stoned.[54] The apostle Paul, likewise, was transformed. Once a ceaseless persecutor of the growing church, he became the chief proselytizer of the Gentiles.

Not everyone gets a second chance to make their life count in this world; however, everyone will have another life in the world to come. On the last day the trump shall resound and the resurrected Christ shall descend (1 Thessalonians 4:16). This time He will come not as a suffering servant lying prostrate in the pool of His own blood, but as King of kings and Lord of lords (see Revelation 19:16). At the sound of His voice, the dead will be resurrected to give an accounting of their lives (John 5:28-29).

Not everyone has been called to be a pastor, but everyone has been called to serve the Master. Whatever our calling, we are to invest our time, talents, and treasures in those things that will last for all eternity. Of one thing I am certain—if twenty-first century Promise Keepers will grasp the significance of the resurrection like the first-century Christians did, our lives will be radically revolutionized. Rather than being microcosms of the culture, we will become change agents. Like a small band of seemingly insignificant believers who succeeded in turning an empire upside down, we will leave a lasting mark on our world. In the end, it all depends on whether we only say we believe in resurrection or whether we *really* believe!

QUESTION 3

Is the Origin of the Bible Divine or Is It Merely Human?

IF THE BIBLE IS MERELY HUMAN IN ORIGIN, ITS TEACHINGS ARE NO MORE AUTHORITATIVE THAN THOSE OF ANY OTHER HOLY BOOK

"The Bible is a product of man, not of God . . . it has evolved through countless translations, additions, and revisions."

LEIGH TEABING, IN DAN BROWN'S *THE DA VINCI CODE*

"Prophecy never had its origin in the will of man, but men spoke from God as they were carried along by the Holy Spirit."

THE APOSTLE PETER (2 PETER 1:21)

The third of the great apologetic issues revolves around the origins of the Bible. Is the Bible divine, or is it merely human in origin? If the Bible is merely the product of man, as *The Da Vinci Code* asserts, it stands in a long line of peers with other holy books. If, on the other

hand, *"men spoke from God as they were carried along by the Holy Spirit"*
(2 Peter 1:21) as the apostle Peter asserts, it is the authority by which to
govern every aspect of our daily lives. In the words of Joshua, *"Do not
let this Book of the Law depart from your mouth; meditate on it day and
night, so that you may be careful to do everything written in it. Then you will
be prosperous and successful"* (Joshua 1:8).

THE SITUATION

Following a tradition begun by George Washington in 1789,
every president of the United States, save one,[55] has been sworn
into office with his right hand on the Bible. Until recently
courtroom witnesses were required to swear or "affirm" to "tell
the truth, the whole truth, and nothing but the truth" with their
hands on the Bible. Such traditions are indicative of a historic
cultural commitment to the moral authority of the Bible.

Today, pluralistic approaches to religious truth, postmodern
literary criticism, and the privatization of religious faith have increasingly relativized and trivialized the Bible in Western society. While some
peoples around the world still await the translation of the Bible into
their own languages, the abundance of translations of the Bible that line

the shelves of Christian and secular bookstores make it possible for us to go to church color-coordinated with our Bibles. Tragically, such over-familiarity has bred under-utilization, which in turn has bred contempt.

On a recent episode of the television show *Penn and Teller: Bull S#ᵃ!*, the Bible was the focus of an hour-long tirade of sarcastic scoffing and disrespectful derision. After an hour of pseudo-scholastic scorn, Penn Jillette, magician and co-host of the show, concluded with the following remarks:

Take some time and put the Bible on your summer reading list. Try to stick with it cover to cover. Not because it teaches history—we've shown you it doesn't. Read it because you'll see for yourself what the Bible is all about. It sure isn't great literature. If it were published as fiction no reviewer would give it a passing grade. There are some vivid scenes and some quotable phrases, but there's no plot, no structure, there's a tremendous amount of filler and the characters are painfully one-dimensional. Whatever you do, don't read the Bible for a moral code. It advocates prejudice, cruelty, superstition, and murder. Read it because we need more atheists, and nothing will get you there faster than reading the damn Bible.[56]

In similar fashion, John Shelby Spong, the former Episcopalian Bishop of Newark, dogmatically asserts that the Bible is full of errors and "irreconcilable contradictions."[57] He asserts that "there are passages in the Gospels that portray Jesus of Nazareth as narrow-minded, vindictive, and even hypocritical."[58] And he generally characterizes those who believe in the inerrancy of Scripture as uniformed and gullible.[59]

THE STAKES

If skeptical secularism is correct, the Bible is at best a collection of interesting historical documents with no real spiritual authority and at worst the manipulative musings of a few maniacal men. If the words of the Bible, though recorded by human authors, were not sovereignly inspired and preserved by God, then the Bible is no more authoritative than the Q'uran of Islam, the Bhagavad Gita of Hinduism, the Pali Canon of Theravada Buddhism, the Lotus Sutra of Mahayana Buddhism, or the Book of Mormon.

Not only so, but if the Bible is merely human in origin, Jesus was mistaken to say to the Father, *"Your word is truth"* (John

17:17). And this was not an isolated remark. Over and over again, Jesus proclaimed the infallibility of Scripture. *"The Scripture cannot be broken,"* He told the unbelieving Jews (John 10:35). And to the crowds he said, *"I tell you the truth, until heaven and earth disappear, not the smallest letter, not the least stroke of a pen, will by any means disappear from the law until everything is accomplished"* (Matthew 5:18). Jesus left no alternative: either the Bible is divine or Jesus is not.

> Over and over again, Jesus proclaimed the infallibility of Scripture. . . . Jesus left no alternative: either the Bible is divine or Jesus is not.

THE SOLUTION

The solution is not merely to accept the Bible on blind faith but to demonstrate that Scripture is rooted and grounded in history and evidence. If we can accomplish this, we can answer a host of objections to the Christian faith by appealing to the Bible. If we cannot, there is no warrant for suggesting that the Bible is anymore authoritative than the Q'uran. To demonstrate that the Bible is divine rather than merely human in origin, I've developed the acronym M-A-P-S— Manuscript evidence, Archeological discoveries, Predictive prophecies, and

Statistical probability. The maps in the backs of our Bibles are an enduring reminder that its details and descriptions are rooted in reality rather than in myths and fables.

MANUSCRIPT EVIDENCE

Because we do not have the original biblical writings (*autographa*) the question is, "How good are the copies?" The answer is that the Bible has stronger manuscript support than any other work of classical literature, including Homer, Plato, Aristotle, Caesar, and Tacitus. There are presently more than five thousand Greek biblical manuscripts (handwritten copies) in existence,[60] and as many as twenty thousand more translations in such languages as Latin, Coptic, and Syriac.

> The Bible has stronger manuscript support than any other work of classical literature, including Homer, Plato, Aristotle, Caesar, and Tacitus.

Incredibly, there's reason to believe that the earliest New Testament manuscript fragments may be dated all the way back to the second half of the first century.[61] This is amazing when you consider that only two manuscripts survive containing the important *Histories* and *Annals* of the first-century historian

Tacitus—and there is a 700-year gap separating the earliest extant copy from the original writing![62] Equally amazing is the fact that the New Testament has been virtually unaltered, as has been documented by scholars who have compared the earliest written manuscripts with manuscripts written centuries later.

The evidence for the enduring accuracy of the Old Testament is also impressive, particularly in light of the discovery of the Dead Sea Scrolls in the late 1940s. These scrolls predate what was previously the earliest extant text (the Masoretic text) by a thousand years. Thus, there is a thousand-year time span in which to determine how well God has preserved His Word. The findings are remarkable. While there are differences in style and spelling, there are no differences in substance.

Furthermore, the reliability of Scripture is confirmed through the eyewitness credentials of the authors. Moses, for example, participated in and was an eyewitness to the remarkable events of the Egyptian captivity, the Exodus, the forty years in the desert, and Israel's final encampment before entering the Promised Land, all of which are accurately chronicled in the Old Testament.[63]

The New Testament has the same kind of eyewitness

attestation. For example, Luke says that he gathered eyewitness testimony and *"carefully investigated everything"* (Luke 1:1-3). John writes, *"That which was from the beginning, which we have heard, which we have seen with our eyes, which we have looked at and our hands have touched—this we proclaim concerning the Word of life"* (1 John 1:1). Likewise, the apostle Peter reminded his readers that the disciples *"did not follow cleverly invented stories"* but *"were eyewitnesses of [Jesus'] majesty"* (2 Peter 1:16).

Finally, secular historians—including Josephus (before A.D. 100), the Roman Tacitus (c. A.D. 120), the Roman Suetonius (c. A.D. 110), and the Roman governor Pliny the Younger (c. A.D. 110)—confirm many of the events, people, places, and customs chronicled in the New Testament. Early church leaders such as Irenaeus, Tertullian, Julius Africanus, and Clement of Rome—all writing before A.D. 250—also shed light on biblical accuracy. Even skeptics agree that the New Testament is a remarkable historical document.[64]

ARCHAEOLOGY

As with the manuscript evidence, archaeology is a powerful witness to the accuracy of biblical documents. Over and over again, comprehensive archaeological fieldwork combined with careful biblical interpretation affirms the reliability of the Bible. It is telling when secular scholars must revise their biblical criticism in light of solid archaeological evidence.

For years, critics dismissed the book of Daniel, partly because there was no evidence that a king named Belshazzar ruled in Babylon during that period. Later archaeological research, however, confirmed that the reigning monarch, Nabonidus, appointed Belshazzar as his coregent while he was waging war away from Babylon.

One of the most well-known New Testament examples concerns the books of Luke and Acts. A biblical skeptic, Sir William Ramsay, was trained as an archaeologist and then set out to disprove the historical reliability of this portion of the New Testament. But through his painstaking Mediterranean archaeo-logical trips, he became a believer as, one after another, the historical allusions of Luke were proved accurate.[65]

Furthermore, archeologists recently discovered a gold mine of archeological nuggets that provide a powerful counter to objections raised by scholars against the biblical account of

Christ's crucifixion and burial. In *U. S. News and World Report*
Jeffrey Sheler highlights the significance of the discovery of the
remains of a man crucified during the first century. This
discovery calls into question the scholarship of liberals who
contend that Jesus was tied rather than nailed to the cross and
that His corpse was likely thrown into a shallow grave and eaten
by wild dogs rather than entombed.[66]

Finally, recent archeological finds have also corroborated
biblical details surrounding the trial that led to the fatal torment of
Jesus Christ—including the existence of Pilate, who ordered
Christ's crucifixion, and the burial grounds of Caiaphas, the high
priest who presided over the religious trials of Christ. As noted by
Sheler, in 1990 a burial chamber dating back to the first century
was discovered two miles south of Temple Mount. "Inside, archae-
ologists found twelve limestone ossuaries. One contained the bones
of a 60-year-old man and bore the inscription *Yehosef bar Qayafa* —
'Joseph, son of Caiaphas.'" Experts believe this almost certainly
refers to Caiaphas the high priest of Jerusalem, who according to
the Gospels ordered the arrest of Jesus, interrogated Him, and
handed Him over to Pontius Pilate for execution.[67]

Regarding Pontius Pilate, Sheler notes that excavations at the seaside ruins of Caesarea Maritima—the ancient seat of the Roman government in Judea—uncovered a first-century inscription confirming that Pilate was the Roman ruler at the time of Christ's crucifixion.[68] Archeologists working at the Herodian theater found a plaque inscribed with the Latin words, *Tiberieum . . . [Pon]tius Pilatus . . . [praef]ectus Juda[ea]e.* "According to experts, the complete inscription would have read, 'Pontius Pilate, the Prefect of Judea, has dedicated to the people of Caesarea a temple in honor of Tiberius.' The discovery of the so-called Pilate Stone has been widely acclaimed as a significant affirmation of biblical history because it confirms that the man depicted in the Gospels as Judea's Roman governor had precisely the responsibilities and authority that the Gospel writers ascribe to him."[69]

As Dr. Nelson Glueck, widely considered to be the greatest modern authority on Israeli archeology, has well said: "No archeological discovery has ever controverted a biblical reference. Scores of archeological findings have been made which confirm in clear outline or in exact detail historical statements in the Bible. And, by the same token, proper evaluation of Biblical descriptions has often led to amazing discoveries."[70] Truly, with every turn of the archaeologist's spade we continue to see evidence for the trustworthiness of the Scriptures.[71]

PREDICTIVE PROPHECY

The Bible records predictions of events that could not be known or predicted by chance or common sense. Surprisingly, the predictive nature of many Bible passages was once a popular argument (by liberals) against the reliability of the Bible. Critics argued that various passages were written later than the biblical texts indicated because they recounted events that happened sometimes hundreds of years later than when they supposedly were written. They concluded that, subsequent to the events, literary editors went back and "doctored" the original texts.

But this is simply wrong. Careful research *affirms* the predictive accuracy of the Scriptures. For example, the previously mentioned book of Daniel (written before 530 B.C.) accurately predicts the progression of kingdoms from Babylon through the Medo-Persian Empire, culminating in the persecution and suffering of the Jews under Antiochus IV Epiphanes, his desecration of the temple, his untimely death, and freedom for the Jews under Judas Maccabeus in 165 B.C.[72]

Old Testament prophecies concerning the Phoenician city of Tyre were fulfilled in ancient times, including prophecies that the city would be opposed by many nations (Ezekiel 26:3); its walls would be destroyed and towers broken down (26:4); and its stones, timbers, and debris would be thrown into the water (26:12). Similar prophecies were fulfilled concerning Sidon (Ezekiel 28:23; Isaiah 23; Jeremiah 27:3-6; 47:4) and Babylon (Jeremiah 50:13, 39; 51:26, 42, 43, 58; Isaiah 13:20, 21).

Because Christ is the culminating theme of the Old Testament and the Living Word of the New Testament, it should not surprise us that prophecies regarding Him outnumber all others. Many of these prophecies would have been impossible for Jesus deliberately to conspire to fulfill—such as His descent from Abraham, Isaac, and Jacob (Genesis 12:3; 17:19; Matthew 1:1-2; Acts 3:25); His birth in Bethlehem (Micah 5:2; Matthew 2:1, 6); His crucifixion with criminals (Isaiah 53:12; Matthew 27:38); the piercing of His hands and feet on the cross (Psalm 22:16; John 20:25); the soldiers' gambling for His clothes (Psalm 22:18; Matthew 27:35); the piercing of His side (Zechariah 12:10; John 19:34) and the fact that His bones were not broken at His death (Psalm 34:20; John 19:33-37); and His burial among the rich (Isaiah 53:9; Matthew 27:57-60).

Moreover, Jesus Himself made predictions about the future, many of which stipulated fulfillment within the lifetimes of those who heard Him prophesy. For example, Jesus predicted His own death and resurrection (John 2:19-22). Jesus also predicted the destruction of Jerusalem and the Jewish Temple (Luke 21)—a prophecy minutely fulfilled by the Roman General Titus in A.D. 70. The Messianic prophesies fulfilled in Christ's life, death and resurrection, as well as Jesus' own predictions, provide an empirically verifiable means of establishing the truth of His claims.

STATISTICS

It is statistically preposterous that the Bible's specific, detailed prophecies could have been fulfilled through chance, good guessing, or deliberate deceit. When you consider some of the improbable prophecies cited above, it seems incredible that skeptics—knowing the authenticity and historicity of the texts—could reject the statistical verdict: The Bible is divine in origin!

Not only so, but consider that the Bible is a collection of sixty-six books, written by forty different human authors in three different languages (Hebrew, Aramaic, and Greek) over a period of 1,500 years, on thousands of different subjects, yet it is unified and consistent throughout. The unfolding message of God's great work in the creation and redemption of all things, through His only Son, the Lord Jesus Christ, is woven throughout the pages of both Old and New Testaments. How is that possible? The individual writers had no idea that their message would eventually be assembled into one Book, yet each work fits perfectly into place with a unique purpose as a component of the whole.

> Manuscript evidence, Archeological discoveries, Predictive prophecies, and Statistical probability demonstrate beyond the peradventure of a doubt the Bible is divine in origin.

The conclusion of the matter is this. Manuscript evidence, Archeological discoveries, Predictive prophecies, and Statistical probability demonstrate beyond the peradventure of a doubt the Bible is divine in origin. Thus the M-A-P-S in your Bibles serve as an enduring reminder that God has spoken. His words are a lamp to our feet and maps to guide us down the pathway of life.

It is precisely because of the strategic importance of the three great apologetic issues that you as a Promise Keeper must be equipped to *"always be prepared to give an answer to everyone who asks you to give the reason for the hope that you have. But do this with gentleness and respect, keeping a clear conscience, so that those who speak maliciously against your good behavior in Christ may be ashamed of their slander"* (1 Peter 3:15-16).

> "No archeological discovery has ever controverted a biblical reference. Scores of archeological findings have been made which confirm in clear outline or in exact detail historical statements in the Bible. And, by the same token, proper evaluation of Biblical descriptions has often led to amazing discoveries."
>
> DR. NELSON GLUECK

We must never lose sight of the fact that apologetics—the defense of the faith—has a dual purpose. On the one hand, it involves pre-evangelism. In a post-Christian world, few people are aware that belief in origins, resurrection and biblical authority is not a blind leap into the dark, but a step into the light.

On the other hand, apologetics involves post-evangelism. During an age in which our faith is under siege, knowing how to defend its reliability serves as a pillar or post to cling to when waves of doubt seek to submerge our faith.

From this point on we will move from major worldview issues to a series of questions pertaining to men as relational beings. In the next three chapters, Tom Fortson will directly address your strategic importance as a man to the proper ordering of our society. Furthermore, he will address the critical concern of isolationism—which is not only dangerous to your spiritual well-being but is potentially devastating to our culture. Finally, Tom will help you understand how you can progress from survival to significance and an unsurpassed *quality* of life. Stick with us, as together we continue preparing for the journey of a lifetime!

QUESTION 4

What Makes Men So Strategic to the Proper Functioning of Society?

THE GOD-GIVEN ROLE OF MEN IS VITAL TO THE PROPER ORDERING OF BOTH THE FAMILY AND SOCIETY

My wife and I are making several design changes in our home now that all of our children have left home as adults, and we recently purchased an electric fireplace with a remote control. Turn the heat up or down. Turn the light on high or low, off or on. The remote does it all, and you don't have to get up. The unit seems to do everything you would ever want a fireplace to do. It even looks like a real fireplace.

The fireplace came with a manual. I wasn't surprised about the manual; I was surprised that it came in three languages. Many men, like me, see things in a simplified manner, so I often bypass the designer's plan. You guessed it: the fireplace did not work the first time. We not only had to go back and read the manual, we had to call the help desk.

Similarly, if we are going to address the issue of what makes men so strategic to the proper functioning of a society, it would be wise to read and study what the Designer had in mind. He has given us the manual called the Bible, which as we have seen is demonstrably divine in origin. Like other manuals, the Bible is meant to be used both *before* we have problems, as well as later when we need a reference to help us fix the broken places in our lives.

> The Bible is meant to be used both before we have problems, as well as later when we need a reference to help us fix the broken places in our lives.

Let me make a few comments about the Bible (our manual for living) that provide insight on the ideas that will come in this chapter. The Bible is:

- Infallible (true)
- Inerrant (without mistakes)
- Complete (states what is needed)
- Authoritative (the Word of God)
- Sufficient (addresses our needs)
- Dynamic (powerful to change lives)

So let's open the Bible and discover what God says . . .

We were created in God's image as part of His creation: *"So God created man in His own image, in the image of God He created him; male and female He created them"* (Genesis 1:27). Throughout scripture, we see God's intent for harmony in interpersonal relationships, equality in personhood and importance, and difference in role and authority.

Throughout history, and in the most diverse cultures, we see God's intent for order and harmony in the family and society. We see man throughout the ages as a protector, provider, mentor, friend, and lover. We can take this for granted, or even argue about it. I would suggest, however, that man's roles are part of the divine plan. We can clearly see the disorder and chaos that result if we don't follow and trust His plan and design.

I want to make a clear statement here. Men and women are equally important to God and equal in value to Him. It is obvious, however, that they are different from each other as are any complimentary pairs. This should exclude all feelings of pride, inferiority or superiority, or the idea that one gender is better or worse than the other. Our roles in marriage and in the church are set forth by God as part of the created order. This is the beauty of the cooperation implied by the expression *"one flesh"*

(Genesis 2:24). The distinction in masculine and feminine roles is ordained by God as part of the created order. You can see this pattern throughout history, culture, geography, and ethnicity. Man is strategic because God made him strategic. Everything God did was, and is, good and is strategic in His divine creation.

Let me address five key strategic roles of men in the family and in society:

- Protector
- Provider
- Mentor
- Friend
- Lover

MAN AS PROTECTOR

"Govern a family as you would cook a small fish—very gently."

CHINESE PROVERB

The stereotypical image of a protector may be that of a big man with a scowl on his face, standing in the front door refusing to allow a weird-looking adolescent to take his teenage daughter to the mall to "hang out." With a few exceptions, protection nowadays is rarely physical combat on behalf of the family. The club-in-hand warrior of the ancient world is now movie stuff.

Being a protector today incorporates the following:

- **Prevention**. Prevention is a key element for a father in being the protector. Keeping your wife and family out of harm's way may be accomplished by setting boundaries or reasonable expectations, like a daughter being home at a reasonable time. Prevention is a matter of the mind.

- **Planning**. Planning establishes the details of leadership in the behaviors and activities of each family member. Planning is like the seatbelt of protection. It should not restrict freedom of movement except in an unexpected and dangerous situation. Planning may take the practical form of buying a safe car, or the alarming task of preparing your children to react appropriately to a kidnapper or pedophile.

- **Preparation**. Preparation is putting the plan into action. This action may be role-playing with your children so they can plan their actions or talk about decision making. It may be talking

with growing children about the results of dangerous choices.
It can be interaction with your family about embracing the
biblical values that guide your family in their personal choices.

- **Precautions**. Precautions are the results of implementing
  "protector assignments." The protector must, first of all, be a
  man of prayer. *"God is our refuge and strength"* (Psalm 46:1).
  Precautions should be practical and tactical like preparing
  adequate security for your home. Like a warning road sign
  before a dangerous curve, precautions place temporary
  behavioral limitations for the family's protection.

- **Persuasion**. That's right! To be an effective protector, a husband
  and dad must have buy-in from the family. A dad needs the
  persuasion of relationship or he will lack the cooperation with
  his leadership that will make his covering as a protector an
  effective one. A friend of mine tells the story of his father using
  the persuasion of character. As a teenager, he and his brother
  were ready to hit the road in their revved-up car. Their dad
  refocused their attention to all the values he represented with
  the following six words: "Boys, remember whose sons you are."
  That quote can also speak to every Christian!

MAN AS PROVIDER

"We make a living by what we get, but we make a life by what we give."
WINSTON CHURCHILL

The principle of a man as a provider was clearly demonstrated to me by my Dad. There were times when I was growing up that he worked three jobs so that our needs would be met. This example did not go unnoticed by his son. I caught it!

We may toil to survive, but what we provide through our hard work is a source of support to our families, our communities, and ourselves. A review of man as the family provider in our culture shows that, until the last thirty years, his responsibility has been to work outside of the home, while his wife has toiled raising the children and taking care of all matters related to the upkeep of the home. Watch a television show from the 1950s or 1960s and you will see an image of the man of the house as the breadwinner—the provider for the family.

The fact is that typical family images change through the years. Whether the man of today is the sole support of the family or part of a two-person working household, he often still provides more than financial security. He works with his wife to provide guidance for their children, setting and enforcing rules to help their children succeed in life.

Outside the home, a man provides a source of support for his friends and extended family. Whether he serves as a counselor for friends having personal difficulties or an advisor to family members who have questions on specific issues, a man uses his knowledge and experience to help others. He is an individual who volunteers at a soup kitchen or answers a hotline, providing solace and support to less-fortunate individuals. He serves as the voice of kindness and compassion, reaching out a hand and providing a degree of hope to people who are facing extremely difficult times in their lives.

MAN AS MENTOR

"How lovely that everyone, great and small, can make their contribution . . . how we can always, always give something, even if it is only kindness."

ANNE FRANK

Even as adults we still need older men to mentor us. Alonzo E. Short, Jr. (Lt. General, ret.) is a three-star General in the U.S. Army, and is a mentor to me. Throughout his military career, he has been a leader of men and women, and he has consistently passed on to me numerous leadership principles he has studied and gained from experience. His timely phone calls with words of both encouragement and caution have been invaluable to me. No matter how busy he is, he takes time to listen. Each of us needs a General to hear us and counsel us.

A recent ad campaign on television, in magazines, and in newspapers asked the question, "Who Mentored You?" The ads provided an array of famous people touting the importance of mentoring. Quincy Jones, Cal Ripken, Jr., Gloria Estefan, Sen. John McCain, and many others talked about the importance mentoring played in their lives and encouraged other adults to become mentors. The government declared January as "National Mentoring Month," with January 26, 2006 designated as "Thank Your Mentor Day" in recognition of the importance one person can play in the life of another.

Mentors can be any significant adult in a person's life. For instance, according to the *"Who Mentored You?"* website (www.whomentoredyou.org), Gen. Colin Powell was mentored by his father; Quincy Jones was mentored by Ray Charles; Helen

Keller was mentored by Anne Sullivan; and Gloria Estefan was mentored by her grandmother. A mentor can be anyone who provides a positive influence on another's life. Gen. Powell states that, even though his father was small in stature, only 5 feet 2 inches tall he was a mighty man in the life's lessons he taught his son. Gen. Powell learned that he should never limit himself by his race or station in life, and credits his successes to the lessons he learned from his father. A father who is also a mentor and a guide plays a vital role in the growth of the child. Mentoring can be received from all venues. Every man must remain aware of his potential to impact a specific person within his family and in his community.

> In all areas of life—family, community, and church—we must accept the task of mentoring others.... We must be teachers and positive role models to those who look to us for guidance, counsel and understanding.

Successful men have the opportunity to let others benefit from their expertise and from their experiences. Near successes also provide a good teaching tool on how to step back, determine what roadblocks have hindered success, and then strive to succeed once again. Success through adversity is a powerful example to impart to an individual who looks to an older, wiser man for guidance.

In all areas of life—family, community, and church—we must accept the task of mentoring others. As children, we learned from the examples of strong, important men and women, and we must pass those lessons on to the next generation. We must be teachers and positive role models to those who look to us for guidance, counsel and understanding. We must foster intentional relationships through which we can help others grow in the grace and knowledge of the Lord, Jesus Christ.

MAN AS FRIEND

> *"Without friends no one would choose*
> *to live, though he had all other goods."*
>
> ARISTOTLE

Friendship is easy to understand but difficult to explain. We have close friends, best friends, trusted friends, childhood friends. Who is your best friend? Is it your spouse or someone you have known for years? What makes friends so special that we like being with them—that being with them makes us feel better? A big part of any relationship is based on actually liking another person.

We all interact with people every day. But, how many of our daily associates are actually friends? We have business colleagues, workplace associates, neighbors. But these individuals may not truly be friends. We may feel friendly toward them, but friendly feelings alone usually do not translate into true friendship. We may claim many friends until we test them and find that we have a few friends and many acquaintances.

Being a friend is so much more than just being friendly. A true friendship involves a high level of trust that is not evident in more casual relationships. Friends are special people. Although we cannot select our family, we can select our friends. We are blessed that we can make friends from diverse populations, not selected because of their gender, race, age, or financial status. Our friends are a reflection of our choices in life. We surround ourselves with friends who not only may share similar interests

> Our friends are a reflection of our choices in life.

with us, but who are honest and forthright. A man knows his innermost secrets are safe when entrusted to a friend. Casual relationships do not exhibit the level of interaction that is evident between friends. Promise Keepers ought to model true, faithful friendship that is based on trust and an unconditional love for other men and women alike.

MAN AS LOVER

> *"Every heart sings a song, incomplete, until another heart*
> *whispers back. Those who wish to sing always find a song.*
> *At the touch of a lover, everyone becomes a poet."*

PLATO

Love is not limited to Valentine's Day, candy, flowers, or diamonds. Neither is love limited to a feeling or an emotion. Rather, love is an attitude of selfless concern for another. Love is expressed through a commitment to seek the best for someone else, putting another's interests above one's own. In romantic love, a man is, by nature, an initiator who sets the climate in relationships. Though his wife may be gifted in this area, she will often hold back, waiting (and hoping) for his lead.

- A man must be a lover, giving himself to his wife.
- A man should be an emotional coach to his daughters, giving them a gauge by which to measure their possible husbands in the future.
- A man should be the example to his sons of how to respect and love a woman with faithfulness, integrity, humble

service, and respect, demonstrating these principles in his love for his wife—their mother. Paul instructs that men are to love their wives as Christ loves the Church (Ephesians 5:25-33), and Christ gave up His own life for His bride!

• A man should be a mentor whose life focuses on instilling these values and the truth of God's perfect love for us—the cognitive side of influence.

Love is loyalty wrapped in action—the soft velvet covering of the strong hand of strength.

"For God so loved the world, that He gave His only begotten Son, that whoever believes in Him shall not perish, but have eternal life."

JESUS OF NAZARETH (JOHN 3:16)

The word "lover" brings to mind Romeo and Juliet, Don Juan, Rudolph Valentino. "Lover" carries the connotation of a romantic relationship between a man and woman. And, this is true to a large extent. However, a man can be a lover in many ways. Romantic love, while very important, is not the beginning or the end.

What is love? What forms does it take? You can love your spouse, love your children, love a cheeseburger with pickles, and love your dog. The words "love" and "lover" are thrown around to describe so many situations. If you listen to poets, songwriters and movie themes, you get the idea that love is easy and being a lover is a piece of cake. A man and a woman meet and a miracle occurs: they fall in love and live happily ever after. The End! However, that happens only in movies or in love songs; it is not real life.

Being a lover in your family, in your relationship with your wife, takes many forms as well. As her lover, a man will listen to what she says, will value her opinions, and will support her physically, emotionally, and materially. Physical love is an important part of the relationship, but the emotional and the psychological sides of love are equally important for a stable relationship. Being a tender, caring man in a committed partnership does not make a man weak or soft. It takes great strength of character to be vulnerable—to be able to show true feelings for another person.

Being a lover goes beyond the relationship with a spouse and family to being a lover of humankind, of the community. A man who is a lover of humankind puts himself on the line to help another person. He considers every man to be his brother and every woman to be his sister. Just as a man is tender and caring for the members of his family, he holds his circle of friends and the members of his community in the same loving and caring fashion.

Is man strategic in the proper functioning of a society? Absolutely, especially in the ways I just described. But, more importantly, his role was—and is—the Creator's design.

QUESTION 5

Is the Danger of Isolation Addressed Through My Involvement In Promise Keepers?

LACK OF ACCOUNTABILITY IS DANGEROUS TO OUR SPIRITUAL WELLBEING

Not a week passes without a media report that announces a family in crisis—torn apart by stress and confusion—a husband or father missing. Newspaper and television reports repeatedly chronicle the actions of men who, from all outward appearances, are responsible, loving husbands and fathers but, in reality, are a mass of internal turmoil. These men retreat into themselves, physically disappear, or, more tragically, harm their spouses and children and vanish, trying to create a new life, free from the disappointments and pressures they felt. In the accounts we hear of these men who went "off the deep end," coworkers, neighbors, and family members usually say the same things: "It was a surprise." "He was a wonderful family man." "I never would have thought he would do something like that." "He was a nice guy." In reality, these men had been suffering for years from isolation—of being disconnected from family, friends, and society. This disconnect is also spiritual. Their relationship with God is in turmoil. In many instances, they may confront God with the pain of their internal chaos and isolation. A man will wring his hands, shake his fists at the sky, and say, like David, *"My God, my God, why have you forsaken me? Far from my deliverance are the words of my groaning. . . . Be not far from me, for trouble is near; For there is none to help"* (Psalm 22:1, 11). It is easier to blame God, blame family members, or blame coworkers than to look introspectively to discover the source of the pain.

Isolation is a common problem in our world. Even in men who don't go off the deep end, isolation is often present and doing unseen harm to them and to their families.

In order to develop an understanding of the isolation in our lives, one must first address the difference between being alone and being lonely. Most people enjoy periods of "aloneness," times when they can reflect on the events of the day, plan for the future, or just enjoy the quiet of being alone. "Loneliness" can occur in a crowded room, in the middle of dinner with family, or on a plane or train. Loneliness relates directly to the lack of meaningful relationships in an individual's life, a feeling of disconnection from family and friends.

Prolonged loneliness can become isolation—a separation from the very support system that should make an individual feel included. While many people enjoy those periods of aloneness, very few enjoy being isolated. Man suffers greatly when he is allowed to remain alone. He feels he has no worth, nobody listens to him, he is not needed, or his presence is not valued. While women are often acutely aware of loneliness and isolation due to their higher social sensitivity, men often are unaware that they are lonely until they are very deeply isolated. Also, men often ignore their feelings of isolation, explaining to themselves that isolation is a part of being a man, having responsibilities, or being a grownup. Men often dismiss their need for deep and meaningful relationships by viewing this need as somehow effeminate.

Scripture addresses the fact that man is best served when he fellowships with others. *"Then the LORD God said, 'It is not good for the man to be alone . . .'"* (Genesis 2:18). Humans are inherently social beings who thrive on being with, and helping, others. When we feel we are not needed, a loss of self worth occurs. An isolated man will look at himself and question his true purpose.

What forces fuel these feelings of loneliness, of isolation? What can be done to dispel loneliness and isolation and help security and connectedness return?

Isolated men are, in most instances, truly frustrated with their lives, their jobs, and their marriages. They feel forced by circumstances, either real or imagined, to isolate themselves from those individuals who could provide the strongest support. Isolated men are becoming a national epidemic, and the fact that these men are allowed to remain isolated, with little hope and little chance to raise themselves from their solitude, is a national disgrace.

Advances in transportation and communication enable us to travel and speak over long distances with ease; however, these great discoveries have changed some of the basic ways we live together. For most of human history the basic community was made up of small tribes or towns. People rarely left family and friends behind. The people you worked with and encountered every day were people who had known you your whole life.

This is no longer the case. Today the American man moves to a new place several times a decade, and may live far from his extended family and old friends. The people he works around are not always the people he lives around, and neither his coworkers nor his neighbors are necessarily his friends. The American ideal of individualism teaches us that success must be accomplished alone. Modern cities are often not large communities, but instead are places where thousands of individuals live in isolation. TV and entertainment distract us from spending time with each other. Instant communication allows us to connect with those we know and love who are thousands of miles away, but it also allows us many opportunities to hide ourselves. Long ago, an isolated man was an exception. Now, isolation is the norm.

The isolated modern man can become a master of disguise. He can hide his pain, failure, and disappointments quite easily.

He can present different versions of himself at his work, in his home, with his neighbors, in his church, and to his family and friends thousands of miles away. This is something that men of earlier generations, who were rooted in tightly knit communities, could not have done so easily. The isolated man at first embraces this isolation because it protects him from showing his weakness and failures to others. But soon he realizes no one knows him or understands him, and he descends into loneliness and despair.

Men who have internalized life's difficulties tend to shun the very support systems that could assist them in rising above their isolation. Psalms of David are often filled with his feelings of loneliness and isolation. *"Look to the right and see; For there is no one who regards me; There is no escape for me; No one cares for my soul"* (Psalm 142:4). Men who are trapped in feelings of solitude and isolation may take great comfort from David's words.

In today's society, even though both husband and wife may work, men are still seen as the main breadwinners, the primary

> The isolated man at first embraces this isolation because it protects him from showing his weakness and failures to others. But soon he realizes no one knows him or understands him, and he descends into loneliness and despair.

support of the family. The man is viewed as the strength or protector of the family unit. When a man is not able to be what he hoped to be, he separates himself and turns inward. This fear of exposing his failures leads to isolation from friends, family, and society in general. He turns his back on life, choosing to remain hidden from everyone. He ponders his difficulties and the fact that he is not able to change any of the problems that have brought him to this crisis. When reviewing the life of this man, special attention should be paid to what is missing from his life. Is it a lack of security? Is it a lack of support? Does he lack self-esteem and strength of character? Why has he allowed his fear to push him so far from his normal life?

When personal or moral failure occurs in the life of a man, he strives to shield those he loves from the problem. As such, this man—this protector—alienates himself from family and friends in an attempt to hide the difficulties in his life. As the protector of the family, his duty is to determine that his wife and children feel safe, protected, and cared for. When he is not able to live up to his own expectations, he isolates himself to hide his failings. He often deludes himself into believing the problems don't really exist. In reality, the hidden problems continue to grow, exacerbated by his isolation. As difficulties increase, the isolated man becomes even more detached from the family and friends he is trying to protect. In the depths of his isolation, the man will realize that his life is out of control.

Many men do not develop close, personal friendships with other men. Men have colleagues, networking opportunities, and golf buddies. These relationships are often superficial in nature. Men tend to shy away from more intimate relationships with other men for a number of reasons, including societal views, mistrust, or lack of interest. Developing close relationships, especially with other men, is difficult because close relationships require vulnerability. Many men tend to surround themselves with an air of mystery to hide their true selves. Developing close relationship also requires adopting a noncompetitive attitude. As men are raised to be competitive in order to survive and provide for their families, doing away with that competitive self is very difficult. So when a man feels out of control, depressed, or lonely, he has no male-to-male support system to which he can turn.

Scripture states in Ecclesiastes, *"For if either of them falls, the one will lift up his companion. But woe to the one who falls when there is not another to lift him up"* (Ecclesiastes 4:10). Nevertheless, an isolated man finds it difficult to ask a friend to assist him. He is truly alone—forced to tough it out without feedback or advice from another male who has faced the same difficulty. Because he has pushed away his family and friends, he feels that he is the only one who has faced this problem.

As a man spirals downward into this pit of isolation, he begins to blame others for his difficulties. For example, problems on the job are caused by coworkers or the boss; difficulties at home are because of an unsupportive spouse or disrespectful children. His isolation turns him into a victim—a man not responsible for the problems that are plaguing him. He might even blame God for his isolation. To admit that turmoil exists, at least in part because of his own actions, is to admit that he is fallible—that he may need to turn to others for support, guidance, and advice.

As a man spirals downward into this pit of isolation, he begins to blame others for his difficulties. . . . To admit that turmoil exists, at least in part because of his own actions, is to admit that he is fallible—that he may need to turn to others for support, guidance, and advice.

Solitude and loneliness have a physical as well as a psychological impact on the man. In the study, *Social Isolation Can Lead to Poor Health Behaviors*, Dr. Eric Louts discovered that men, especially older men who have adopted a socially isolated lifestyle, suffer from health problems at a much greater rate than do men who have positive support systems (*Medscape*, 2003.) Strong support systems, faith in God, and the desire to become a productive member of society may aid the social isolationist's recovery of emotional and physical health. The desire to recover, however, must come from the man himself. He must take responsibility for his isolation, reclaim his life, and once again be the man that he was before crises drove him into solitude. In order to recover from this feeling of separation, he must take responsibility for driving away his support. He needs to turn to God and His Word to help him through stressful and fearful times, whether or not he has a strong support system.

The isolated man may, at first, feel unable to escape the walls he has built around himself. *"A man who isolates himself seeks his own desire; he rages against all wise judgment"* (Proverbs 18:1 NKJV). The apostle Paul reflects the feeling of isolation when he says, *"but all deserted me"* (2 Timothy 4:16). He understood how abandoned a man may feel when he is isolated from friends and family. He feels deserted—feels that no person understands his turmoil, his desperation, and maybe even his shame. David writes in Psalm 69:20, *"Reproach has broken my heart and I am so sick. And I looked for sympathy, but there was none, and for comforters, but I found none."* These words embody the aloneness felt by the man whose failures are hidden from his family and friends. He finds no comfort because there are no comforters to understand his confusion and fear and assist him with his problems. His isolation from

Strong support systems, faith in God, and the desire to become a productive member of society may aid the social isolationist's recovery of emotional and physical health. The desire to recover, however, must come from the man himself. He must take responsibility for his isolation, reclaim his life, and once again be the man that he was before crises drove him into solitude.

any support system pushes him farther and farther from help. He begins to feel desperate. This desperation may even result in abandonment of family, suicide, or violence. If this man had other men in his life who had faced similar difficulties, men with whom he could share his heart, he would know where to find counsel and compassion. He would also know that he needs to reestablish his relationship with God and be directed by the teachings of Christ.

As a Promise Keeper, it is necessary for each man to recognize the signs of isolation in others and provide support and understanding. We offer a community of accountability, brotherhood, and encouragement to men who suffer in isolation. As a Promise Keepers man, through the power of the Holy Spirit, breaks down the barriers he has put up against his family and his friends and seeks to restore his relationship with God, the support of the Promise Keepers network can help him open up, learn to trust again, and begin the healing process. Promise Keepers members should be prepared to recognize a man's despair and potential isolation and step in to offer help. We should not wait to be asked for help—we should be there with open hands and open hearts to help guide individuals toward a deeper dependence on and faith in their Creator and away from isolation and depression. With a support system such as that provided by Promise Keepers, a man would know, without question, that he had brothers to whom he could turn. He would be greeted with kindness and understanding and would be helped and supported by a network designed to provide support for men who are slipping into isolation and separateness.

As a Christ-centered organization, Promise Keepers is dedicated to introducing men to Jesus Christ as their Savior and Lord and helping men grow as Christians. Through strong Christian values and an unshakable commitment to the *Seven Promises*, Promise Keepers stands ready to help any man who has a desire to grow and thrive in the teaching of the Lord. When physical, emotional, or social downturns occur in the life of a Promise Keeper, he knows, without question, that his Promise Keepers brothers will be his strongest human supporters and will help him reconnect with society and with his family.

Think of what a mighty testament such a man will be to the power of God and to the support of his Promise Keepers brothers. During future difficulties, he will remember that God will always be by his side—through the Word and through His servants. *"Be strong and courageous . . . for the LORD your God is the one who goes with you. He will not fail you or forsake you"* (Deuteronomy 31:6). Remembering that God is always there—in his own heart, in his friends and family, and through his support structure—will help keep a man from the depths of isolation and propel him back into his life—his life in Christ.

QUESTION 6

How Can I Go From Survival to Significance?

WHERE THERE IS NO VISION THE PEOPLE PERISH

Turn on the television and you will find *Survivor*, *The Great Race*, and *Fear Factor*. These and so many other television shows are based on being the best, being the winner, being the survivor. Moreover, the winner of each challenge and competition is rewarded with money and fame. Although these programs tout character building and camaraderie, few competitors would participate without the incentive of winning big bucks and fifteen minutes of fame. Many of these competitors have not learned the real challenge in life is to go beyond survival to significance—making a positive impact in one's own life and in the lives of others.

Survival is easy; significance is tough.

STRENGTH FOR SIGNIFICANCE

Many feel that the act of survival accomplishes life's great challenge. If a person is alive, then he or she is surviving. Survival may not always be pretty or comfortable, but it is what it is—continued existence to fight another day. In the near past, each of us has encountered issues such as financial difficulties, a marriage in crisis, children who are troubled, or job difficulties. In addition to the tools necessary for surviving such upheavals, we need to develop the skills that will shape our responses to adversity into models that benefit others. Trials and tribulations will make or break a man, but God has equipped us with the tools to transcend mere survival, allowing us to grow and, ultimately, to benefit others. As Paul said, *"Therefore, take up the full armor of God, so that so that you will be able to resist in the evil day, and having done everything, to stand firm"* (Ephesians 6:13).

> Trials and tribulations will make or break a man, but God has equipped us with the tools to transcend mere survival, allowing us to grow and, ultimately, to benefit others.

The merit of a man may be gauged by his response to difficulties. Just surviving is the man who is seen wringing his hands in fear, shaking his fist at God, and walking, downtrodden, through the rest of his life. This is the face of mere survival: struggling through tough times without holding fast to God's Word and trying to rectify difficulties without God's help. David wrote, *"Though I walk in the midst of trouble, You will revive me; You will stretch forth Your hand against the wrath of my enemies, and Your right hand will save me"* (Psalm 138:7). If you put your faith in God during times of adversity, God will strengthen you to do far more than just survive.

A CASE STUDY: TWO EXAMPLES

The Bible relates many stories that transcend survival. The story of Noah in Genesis is a case in point. God determined that man was too violent and wicked to continue to exist, saying that He would *"blot out man whom I have created from the face of the land, from man to animals to creeping things and to birds of the sky; for I am sorry that I have made them"* (Genesis 6:7). However, Noah gained favor with God and was charged with building the ark that would result in the survival of mankind. As the earth dried, God commanded Noah to return all men and beasts to the earth. In thanks to a gracious God, *"Noah built an altar to the*

Lord, and took of every clean animal and of every clean bird and offered burnt offerings on the altar. The Lord smelled the soothing aroma; and the Lord said to Himself, 'I will never again curse the ground on account of man, for the intent of man's heart is evil from his youth; and I will never again destroy every living thing, as I have done'" (Genesis 8:20-21). Though we often face trials and stressors that are part of life, we must remember to thank God for His patience, His generosity, and His love. If God is not the center of our lives, we will not move from survival to significance in the lives of others.

The apostle Paul lived by example; he lived what he spoke, following the teachings of Christ and challenging others to do likewise. *"Therefore I exhort you, be imitators of me. Be imitators of me, just as I also am of Christ"* (1 Corinthians 4:16; 11:1). We, like Paul, should live the life of which we speak. We can demonstrate that life is more than comforts, fame, and fortune, and that life without Christ in complete control is empty existence—survival and nothing more. It is impossible to maintain fellowship with others if we do not live the words we speak.

HAVING MEANING IN LIFE

Think back a few years to the people with whom you have come in contact. Could you have helped make a life better? Made someone feel significant? Were your actions responsive and responsible? John wrote, *"But whoever has the world's goods, and beholds his brother in need and closes his heart against him, how does the love of God abide in him? Little children, let us not love with word or with tongue, but in deed and truth"* (1 John 3:17-18). Daily we are to serve as positive examples to all whom we encounter. We cannot ignore those who may need our assistance even when the circumstances are inconvenient or untimely for us. Each man needs to accept his role in helping his fellow man. Are we not our brother's keepers? In Genesis, *"the LORD said to Cain, 'Where is Abel your brother?' And he said, 'I do not know. Am I my brother's keeper?'"* (Genesis 4:9). Cain's disrespectful words implied that he had no responsibility for the welfare of his brother. He had killed Abel, and his heart was hardened.

Today, we often harden our hearts to others because we are overwhelmed by tragedy. Review the events that followed the recent hurricane disasters along the Gulf Coast. Initially, people reached out to the evacuees, opening their hearts, homes, and wallets. Now, as action gives way to inertia, generosity is being replaced by a hardening of people's hearts to the misfortunes of others. Regardless of where the fault lies, we must not harden our hearts. We must continue to reach out to help those in need.

DIRECTION FROM GOD

God charges us with living His Word, speaking His Word, and serving as an example of His grace. We can use the words of James as a guide in fellowshipping with others: *"If a brother or sister is without clothing and in need of daily food, and one of you says to them, 'Go in peace, be warmed and be filled,' and yet you do not give them what is necessary for their body, what use is that? Even so faith, if it has no works, is dead, being by itself"* (James 2:15-17). Our actions speak much louder than our words. Failure to follow words like "I will help" or "I understand" or "I'll pray for you" with appropriate actions is hypocrisy. When Paul spoke to the Colossians, he advised them, *"Conduct yourselves with wisdom toward outsiders, making the most of the opportunity. Let your speech always be with grace, as though seasoned with salt, so that you will*

know how you should respond to each person (Colossians 4:5, 6).
Paul reminds us that we should live in a manner that reflects our
words. Moreover, our words should mirror our lives—honest,
encouraging, and charitable.

As Promise Keepers, we present ourselves in a certain
manner. A Promise Keeper lives out *Seven Promises:*

1. to honor Jesus Christ through worship, prayer and obedience
    to God's Word;

2. to pursue vital relationships with a few other men, understanding
    that he needs brothers to help him keep his promises;

3. to practice spiritual, moral, ethical, and sexual purity;

4. to build strong marriages and families through love, protection
    and biblical values;

5. to support the mission of his church by honoring and praying
    for his pastor and by actively giving his time and resources;

6. to reach beyond any racial and denominational barriers to
    demonstrate the power of biblical unity;

7. to influence this world, being obedient to the Great
    Commandment and the Great Commission.

It is our charge to pursue relationships with men that will be beneficial in helping these men, our brothers, walk a Christian path, so that they in turn, will encourage other men along that same path.

We must be aware that our actions as Promise Keepers are viewed and judged by others. We should always strive to lead lives that reflect our mission. We are to "ignite and unite men to be passionate followers of Jesus Christ" realizing that, as we fellowship with men, we are also charged to set a positive example of going beyond just surviving. Each man is the sum of his experiences meshed with the love of God and a duty to help others. How we face and conquer adversity can strengthen us and lead to an even stronger belief in God.

> Each man is the sum of his experiences meshed with the love of God and a duty to help others. How we face and conquer adversity can strengthen us and lead to an even stronger belief in God.

I challenge you to use your past as a library where you get information, not a house where you relive and regret events and mistakes. Reference your past, examine how you have responded to situations and individuals in your life, and determine what improvements need to be made. As you go through life—surviving daily challenges—you should continually examine yourself. You live and project a certain image that others watch and may try to emulate. Your experiences should serve as examples that encourage each person with whom you fellowship as they chart their own course through life. Determine to take every opportunity to be a positive force in the lives of others. Every contact

> Use your past as a library where you get information, not a house where you relive and regret events and mistakes.

represents an opportunity to be a significant and positive influence in the life of a man who otherwise might not seek and receive assistance. Your influence may bring another brother closer to Christ and open his eyes to the truth that life is so much more than surviving.

A Christ-centered life is filled with endless possibilities. Each of us needs to go to that library that is our past and look through the shelves of our personal history. How have we overcome obstacles and stumbling blocks on our way to maturity? Where have we succeeded on our own and where have we needed the help of others? How many times has God proven Himself to be the guiding force in our life? How many times have we said,

"Thank You, God"? Answers to questions like these reveal our persona—our being—identifying personal resources that can help other men on their life's path. And when we sit back at the end of a long day and relax in front of the television, we know that "reality" shows are not reality at all. Making a significant impact in another's life, going beyond mere survival and realizing one's true purpose—that is reality.

QUESTION 7

Why Is It So Crucial for Promise Keepers Men to Develop an Eternal Perspective?

It's an incredible con job, when you think of it, to believe something now in exchange for life after death. Even corporations, with all their reward systems, don't try to make it posthumous.

GLORIA STEINEM

Do not store up for yourselves treasures on earth, where moth and rust destroy, and where thieves break in and steal. But store up for yourselves treasures in heaven, where moth and rust do not destroy, and where thieves do not break in and steal. For where your treasure is, there your heart will be also.

JESUS CHRIST

If ever there was a man who lived with eternity in mind, it was the apostle Paul. While he was saved by God's grace through faith in Jesus Christ alone, he recognized that he was saved unto good works. Thus while Paul did not work *for* his salvation, he did work *from* his salvation. That is precisely the point he was driving at in one of his letters to the Corinthians. Pressing the analogy of athletics, he wrote, *"Do you not know that in a race all the runners run, but only one gets the prize? Run in such a way as to get the prize. Everyone who competes in the games goes into strict training. They do it to get a crown that will not last; but we do it to get a crown that will last forever"* (1 Corinthians 9:24–25). Thus says Paul, *"I do not run like a man running aimlessly; I do not fight like a man beating the air. No, I beat my body and make it my slave so that after I have preached to others, I myself will not be disqualified for the prize"* (vv. 26–27).

THE SITUATION

The prize Paul strove for was not earthly. It was eternal. In sharp contrast, the baubles we often pursue have little lasting value. A recent television commercial advertising a new pickup truck ran through a long list of luxury features including an extended cab with leather seats, multiple climate controls, noise–reducing technology, a DVD player, and, of course, increased power. While nothing about this new luxury truck seemed particularly fascinating or extraordinary, I was struck by the slogan at the end of the commercial. Just as the commercial was winding up and the list of luxurious features was leaving its mark on an impressionable TV audience, the announcer concluded by explaining, "It's not more than you need, just more than you're used to." Translated, "You *need* this new toy!"

Fact is we live in a culture where we are constantly bombarded by billboards, catalogues, TV and radio commercials that aim to convince us that, no matter how well off we are, we deserve—or as in the case of the truck ad, we *need*—more and better stuff all the time. Not only are we told to amass material things, such as bigger and better houses and cars, we are also told that it is justifiable to go to extremes of manipulation, backstabbing, and hypocrisy to attain higher positions of authority in the workplace or respectability among our peers. Still further, we must achieve greater individual happiness in relationships, even if that involves breaking the vows of marriage or walking out on the responsibility of parenting when the going gets tough.

Tragically, this culturally pervasive individualism mixed with a heavy dose of materialism and victim mentality has not only infiltrated the culture, but it has invaded the church as well. Having lost the ability to think biblically, postmodern believers have all too quickly transformed from cultural change–agents and initiators into cultural conformists and imitators. Pop–culture beckons and postmodern believers seem all too anxious to take the bait—an empty bauble for eternal treasure. We would do well to heed these words of C. S. Lewis: "If you read history you will find that the Christians who did most for the present world were just those who thought most of the next. The Apostles themselves, who set on foot the conversion of the Roman Empire, the great men who built up the Middle Ages, the English Evangelicals who abolished the Slave Trade, all left their mark on earth, precisely because their minds were occupied with heaven. It is because Christians have largely ceased to think of the other world that they have become so ineffective in

> Postmodern believers have all too quickly transformed from cultural change–agents and initiators into cultural conformists and imitators. Pop–culture beckons and postmodern believers seem all too anxious to take the bait–an empty bauble for eternal treasure.

this. *Aim at heaven and you will get earth 'thrown in': aim at earth and you will get neither."* [73]

It is important to remember that while some believers may experience a measure of physical comfort this side of death, being Kingdom Christians may mean living under very difficult conditions as did the Apostle Paul who warned in 2 Timothy 3:12: *"In fact, everyone who wants to live a godly life in Christ Jesus will be persecuted."* Though direct physical persecution is rare in the West due to the widespread protection of religious liberty, developing an eternal perspective means standing ready to be persecuted if necessary. Viewing the world through an eternal perspective also means standing in solidarity with our Christian brothers and sisters around the world who are currently being jailed, tortured, and killed on account of their faith. We must not become so complacent in the comforts of our religious liberties that we forget to pray for and publicly defend our brothers and sisters who are suffering.

> The issue of eternal perspective, of being a Kingdom Christian is one of mindset. It is about conforming to the will of God. God's good and perfect will may contain blessing and suffering, prosperity as well as adversity.

The issue of eternal perspective, of being a Kingdom Christian is one of mindset. It is about conforming to the will of God. God's good and perfect will may contain blessing and suffering, prosperity as well as adversity.

Any cultural conformity except that illustrated by the Apostle Paul—*"I have become all things to all men, that I might by all possible means save some"*(1 Corinthians 9:22), which describes not changing who we are but how we relate to others evangelistically—reflects a lack of Christian maturity and a lack of eternal perspective. When you have an eternal perspective you realize that service in God's kingdom is not always comfortable or easy, though it is always fulfilling. Because following Christ is not always a walk in the park, but often an arduous cross–bearing trek to Golgotha, it can be easy to fall into the trap of believing that the world has something better to offer. When we lose our sense of eternal perspective we can easily become obsessed with the temporary pleasures of this world and begin to live for material wealth or peer respectability rather than for our Lord, Jesus Christ.

But, as Dallas Willard has observed, "If we do not treasure earthly goods we must be prepared to be treated as more or less crazy. This is also true if we escape the delusions of respectability and so are not governed by the opinions of those around us."[74] As we attempt to develop an eternal perspective and fight the pressure of cultural conformity, we must heed Paul's timely exhortation:

> *Therefore, I urge you, brothers, in view of God's mercy, to offer your bodies as living sacrifices, holy and pleasing to God—this is your spiritual act of worship. Do not conform any longer to the pattern of this world, but be transformed by the renewing of your mind. Then you will be able to test and approve what God's will is—his good, pleasing and perfect will* (Romans 12:1–2).

THE STAKES

Without an eternal perspective, not only will we miss opportunities to participate in God's sovereign work in this world, we will also miss out on the abundantly good life God desires for each and every one of His children. This good life is characterized by the rewards God's faithful servants will receive in heaven and the abundance of eternal life that they will know this side of death as they experience the blessings of the

> What we do during this earthly sojourn counts and will impact what we do throughout eternity.

kingdom of God on earth. What we do during this earthly sojourn counts and will impact what we do throughout eternity.

REWARDS IN HEAVEN

Heavenly rewards are not often the subject of contemporary sermons; they were, however, a constant theme in the sermons of Christ and the letters of the apostles.

First, the imagery of crowns was used by the apostles to symbolize the rewards awaiting the righteous in heaven. In a letter to Timothy, Paul urges his young protégé to train himself for righteousness in the same way that a runner trains for a race. You can almost hear him gasping for breath as he cries out, *"I have fought the good fight, I have finished the race, I have kept the faith. Now there is in store for me the* crown of righteousness, *which the Lord, the righteous Judge, will award to me on that day—and not only to me, but also to all who have longed for his appearing"* (2 Timothy 4:7–8). Similarly, Peter promises that when Jesus Christ returns we *"will receive the* crown of glory *that will never fade away"* (1 Peter 5:4), an enduring reminder that we are *"a chosen people, a royal priesthood, a holy nation, a people belonging to God"* (1 Peter 2:9).

As Peter urges us to live with an eternal perspective, so that we will receive the crown of glory, James urges us to live with perseverance so that we may receive the crown of life. Says James, *"Blessed is the man who perseveres under trial, because when he has stood the test, he will receive the* crown of life *that God has promised to those who love him"* (James 1:12).

Furthermore, Jesus explicitly points to *degrees* of reward that will be given for faithful service, self–sacrifice, and suffering. In his most famous sermon, Christ repeatedly referred to rewards. In concluding the Beatitudes he said, *"Blessed are you when people insult you, persecute you and falsely say all kinds of evil against you because of me. Rejoice and be glad, because great is your* reward *in heaven"* (Matthew 5:11–12). In the parable of the talents (Matthew 25:14–30) Jesus suggests that varying degrees of faithfulness on earth will be honored by varying degrees of rewards in heaven. Christ also communicates the concept of rewards in his prophetic pronouncement in the very last chapter of the very last book of the Bible. Says Christ, *"Behold, I am coming soon! My reward is with me, and I will give to everyone according to what he has done"* (Revelation 22:12). And this is not a singular statement—in Matthew, the Savior says, *"the Son of Man is going to come in his Father's glory with his angels, and then he will reward each person according to what he has done"* (Matthew 16:27).

Finally, though the basis of our salvation is the finished work of Christ, Christians can erect a building of rewards upon that foundation. As Paul puts it, *"no one can lay any foundation other than the one already laid, which is Jesus Christ. If any man builds on this foundation using gold, silver, costly stones, wood, hay or*

Some Christians will be resurrected with precious little to show for the time they spent on earth.

straw, his work will be shown for what it is, because the Day will bring it to light. It will be revealed with fire, and the fire will test the quality of each man's work. If what he has built survives, he will receive his reward. If it is burned up, he will suffer loss; he himself will be saved, but only as one escaping through the flames" (1 Corinthians 3:11–15).

Paul here illustrates the sober reality that some Christians will be resurrected with precious little to show for the time they spent on earth—they *"will be saved, but only as one escaping through the flames."* This conjures up images of people escaping burning buildings with little more than the charred clothes upon their backs. Likewise, Christ, whose eyes are *"like blazing fire"* (Revelation 1:14) will incinerate the work of those who built monuments to themselves using *"wood, hay or straw"* (1 Corinthians 3:12). This will be the lot of even the most visible Christian leaders whose perspectives were selfish and short–sighted rather than selfless and eternal.

Conversely, those who build selflessly upon the foundation of Christ using *"gold, silver and costly stones"* (1 Corinthians 3:12) will receive enduring rewards. Indeed, a selfless Christian layman who labors in virtual obscurity will hear the words he has longed for throughout his life: *"Well done, good and faithful servant! You have been faithful with a few things; I will put you in charge of many things. Come and share your master's happiness!"* (Matthew 25:21).

LIFE TO THE FULL

While faithful service in this life will be rewarded in the resurrection, living with an eternal perspective is also the only way to experience the kind of abundant Kingdom life for which God designed us. Speaking of the children of God Jesus announced, *"I have come that they may have life, and have it to the full"* (John 10:10).

During His ministry on earth Jesus described just how full life lived according to the power of God's kingdom could be. The kind of life available to those who live with eternity in view is characterized by a lack of worry and anxiety over what to eat and what to wear (Matthew 6:25–34) and by an assurance that what they ask for according to the will of God will be granted to them (Matthew 7:7–12). He promised rest for the weary (Matthew 11:28–30) and a firm foundation on which we may ground our lives (Matthew 7:24–27). This abundant life is also one in which we are set free from the bondage of our enslavement to sin (John 8:34–36).

> While faithful service in this life will be rewarded in the resurrection, living with an eternal perspective is also the only way to experience the kind of abundant Kingdom life for which God designed us.

As Dallas Willard has profoundly noted:

[T]he treasure we have in heaven is also something very much available to us now. We can and should draw upon it as needed, for it is nothing less than God himself and the wonderful society of his kingdom even now interwoven in my life. . . . What is most valuable for any human being, without regard to an afterlife, is to be part of this marvelous reality, God's kingdom now. Eternity is now ongoing. I am now leading a life that will last forever. Upon my treasure in the heavens I now draw for present needs.[75]

Paul is a great example of someone who, despite difficult circumstances, learned to live the kind of full life available to those whose minds have been transformed and who now view their temporary trials and tribulations in light of eternity. Says Paul:

I have learned to be content whatever the circumstances. I know what it is to be in need, and I know what it is to have plenty. I have learned the secret of being content in any and every situation, whether well fed or hungry, whether living in plenty or in want. I can do everything through him who gives me strength (Philippians 4:11–13).

Only by living life with an eternal perspective can we truly experience the great rewards in store for us in heaven and the abundant eternal life available to us even now.

THE SOLUTION

As evidenced by the scriptural promises of heavenly rewards and abundance of life, the point is not that we should renounce desire altogether, as some schools of Buddhism teach, but that we should desire the good life that God has in store for those who love Him, not the life of selfishness and greed offered to those who love the world. How then does one develop the kind of eternal perspective necessary to be able to distinguish the good things of God from the enticing pleasures of the world? Two thousand years ago Jesus recognized the importance of developing an eternal perspective, and He taught and lived out the disciplines necessary to be transformed by the renewing of your mind.

> Only by living life with an eternal perspective can we truly experience the great rewards in store for us in heaven and the abundant eternal life available to us even now.

First, the best way to begin developing an eternal perspective is by saturating our lives with the Word of God. As I have often said, we must get into the Word of God and allow the Word of God to get into us. In the pages of the Bible we come face to face with the eternal character of God and with His sovereign plan for the redemption of humanity that He has been working out since the beginning of time. Jesus modeled this kind of devotion to the Word of God, and when faced with the temptations of the devil, Jesus was able to stand firm in obedience to His Father by relying on the eternal truths of the Sword of the Spirit (Matthew 4:1–11).

Furthermore, we begin to view this world with an eye toward eternity when, shedding our concern for wealth and respectability, we selflessly focus on the interests of others and sacrificially care for those in need. Jesus taught that at the Day of Judgment those who fed the hungry, gave drink to the thirsty, clothed the naked, cared for the sick, and visited those in prison will be rewarded as if they had done these things for the Lord Himself (Matthew 25:31–40). Those who fail to care for the needy will be judged as though they neglected the Lord Himself (vv. 41–46). As James put it, *"Religion that God our Father accepts is this: to look after orphans and widows in their distress and to keep oneself from being polluted by the world"* (James 1:27). But, as Jesus warns, *"when you give to the needy, do not let your left hand know what your right hand is doing, so that your giving may be in secret. Then your Father, who sees what is done in secret will reward you"* (Matthew 6:3–4).

Focusing on meeting the needs of others less fortunate than ourselves is not only a biblical mandate, it is also the best cure for the victim mentality and self–pity by which we can become so easily consumed when we fail to view our temporary trials in light of God's eternal purposes.

Finally, we develop an eternal perspective when we pray in the secret place. Luke tells us that *"Jesus often withdrew to lonely places and prayed"* (Luke 5:16). Jesus warned that the Pharisees who prayed for public recognition and respectability had already received their reward in full. Jesus taught that our concern should not be for the opinions of men, but for the approval of our heavenly Father. Thus, if you want to develop the kind of eternal perspective that leads to abundant living both now and for all eternity, *"'when you pray, go into your room, close the door and pray to your Father, who is unseen. Then your Father, who sees what is done in secret, will reward you'"* (Matthew 6:6).

Christ's message is crystal clear. Rather than fixate on earthly vanities, such as the admiration of men, we ought to focus on such eternal verities as the approval of the Master. He warned His followers not to store up for themselves *"treasures on earth, where moth and rust destroy, and where thieves break in and steal"* (Matthew 6:19). Instead, said Jesus, we should store up *"treasures in heaven, where moth and rust do not destroy, where thieves do not break in and steal"* (v. 20). The rewards for a life of devotion to the Word of God, care for the needy, and faithful prayer in the secret place involve not only enlarged responsibilities but enhanced spiritual capacities. Just like the capacity for enjoying music is greatly enhanced when one masters a musical instrument, the work we do here and now will greatly enhance our capacity for enjoying eternity.

Rather than conforming to culture, Promise Keepers must seek to transform culture by developing an eternal perspective and by living for eternal heavenly rewards and treasures instead of the temporary trappings of this tarnished world.

Afterword

A new unity is growing in the body of Christ. This unity
results from new friendships that develop into deeper relationships. One of my newer and deepening relationships is my
appreciation and love for Hank Hanegraaff. Together, as we
collaborated on this book, we developed more value and understanding in our personal relationship.

In a broader sense, for all of us in the body of Christ, deeper
friendships promote clearer communication, frank discussions,
accountability, inspiration, encouragement
and a host of additional benefits. When we
know each other better we get through
"style and language" to "substance and
heart." Knowing someone's heart will help
one to resonate with the statement attributed to St. Augustine:
"In essentials—unity, in non–essentials—liberty, but in all
things—charity."

Oneness of heart is not a guarantee that we agree on every

> In essentials–unity, in
> non–essentials–liberty,
> but in all things–charity.
>
> ST. AUGUSTINE

detail, but that we seek the common ground of brotherhood and
ministry, and, as the apostle Paul in Philippians 3:15–16 says:

> *"All of us who are mature should take such a view of things.*
> *And if on some point you think differently, that, too, God will*
> *make clear to you. Only let us line up to what we have already*
> *attained."*

When the apostle was speaking, there was no question who
was mature and who still needed to "line up." When interpretation of scriptures divide us, it is best to be gracious and, as the
apostle says, "God will make clear to you." This does not stifle
discussion, research, or debate, but it covers them in prayer and
illuminates them by the Spirit of God.

The thrust of this book is a focus on questions whose answers
can give confidence as to our standing as Christian men. Each of
us is called to "live up to what we have already attained." We have
attained both a common faith in Christ and, as this book has
reminded us, some foundational underpinnings of a Christian
world view that support our premise. The chapters fall into two
categories: those of deepening understanding (Chapters One,

Two, Three, and Seven) and those of application (Chapters Four, Five, and Six). The topics of planet earth created by God (Chapter One), the resurrection of Jesus Christ (Chapter Two), the origins of a divinely inspired Bible (Chapter Three), and a life lived with an eternal perspective (Chapter Seven), give us a solid footing. These foundations come to life as a man realizes that God made him to be strategic in His plan (Chapter Four), wants to protect him from isolationism to live interdependent in Christ's body (Chapter Five), and desires that he move in maturity from survival to significance (Chapter Six).

The mission of Promise Keepers is to "ignite and unite men to passionately follow Jesus Christ;" Hank's Kingdom role, as apologist, is to address details of our faith and equip believers to offer cogent answers for the hope that they have in Christ. Both of these roles are important, and neither is easy to position—unity without compromising truth, detail without producing division or being doctrinaire. We all need grace to allow the Lord, through each other, to stretch

> We all need grace to allow the Lord, through each other, to stretch and inform us, just as He stretches and informs us by His Word and Holy Spirit.

and inform us, just as He stretches and informs us by His Word and Holy Spirit.

So, how about you? Hank and I have experienced a journey together that has produced a strong bond of friendship and faithfulness. Our individual Christian walks have grown, our ministry experiences have been enhanced, and our understanding of Kingdom challenges and issues has been enlarged.

Together, Hank and I ask you this final question:

As Promise Keepers, brothers in Christ,
do we not owe it to one another to cultivate
deep relationships, brother to brother?

WE ENCOURAGE YOU TO TAKE THE NEXT STEP!
LET US LIVE UP TO HIS EXPECTATIONS!

ACKNOWLEDGEMENT

Some of the material in *Seven Questions of a Promise Keeper* has been adapted from Hank Hanegraaff's previously published books.

From Thomas Nelson Publishers:

The Bible Answer Book, Volume 1	*Fatal Flaws*
Counterfeit Revival	*The Prayer of Jesus*
The Covering	*Resurrection*
The FACE	*The Third Day*

From Tyndale House Publishers:
The Da Vinci Code: Fact or Fiction?

NOTES

Introduction

[1] C.S. Lewis, *Mere Christianity* (New York: Collier Books, 1952), 36, emphasis added.

Chapter One: Privileged Planet

[2] J.P. Moreland, ed., *The Creation Hypothesis* (Downers Grove, Ill.: IVP, 1994), 33.

[3] William Dembski, *Intelligent Design* (Downers Grove, Ill.: IVP, 1999), 103.

[4] Dembski, *Intelligent Design*, 103.

[5] Arthur S. Eddington, *The Nature of the Physical World* (New York: Macmillan, 1930), 74.

[6] Julian Huxley, *Essays of a Humanist* (Middlesex, England: Penguin Books), 130.

[7] Letter from Charles Darwin to W. Graham, 3 July 1881, in Francis Darwin, ed, *Life and Letters*, vol. 1 (London, 1887), 316, as quoted in Gertrude Himmelfarb, *Darwin and the Darwinian Revolution* (New York: W. W. Norton & Co., 1968), 416.

[8] The quote continues: "At the same time the anthropomorphous apes...will no doubt be exterminated. The break between man and his nearest allies will then be wider, for it will intervene between man in a more civilized state, as we may hope, even than the Caucasian, and some ape as low as a baboon, instead of as now between the negro or Australian and the gorilla." (Charles Darwin, *The Descent of Man*, chapter VI "On the Affinities and Genealogy of Man," section "On the Birthplace and Antiquity of Man." In Robert Maynard Hutchins, ed., *Great Books of the Western World*, vol. 49, *Darwin* (Chicago: Encyclopaedia Britannica, 1952), 336.

[9] Commenting on the subtitle of *The Origin of Species*, the historian Gertrude Himmelfarb writes, "Darwin, of course, took 'races' to mean varieties or species; but it was no violation of his meaning to extend it to human races, these being as much subject to the struggle for existence and survival of the fittest as plant and animal varieties. Darwin himself, in spite of his aversion to slavery, was not averse to the idea that some races were more fit than others, and that this fitness was demonstrated in human history." (Himmelfarb, *Darwin and the Darwinian Revolution*, 416).

[10] "Agnostic," coined from Greek, literally means "someone with a privation of knowledge." The term was suggested by Huxley in 1869 to refer to one who thinks it is impossible to know whether there is a God or a future life, or anything beyond material phenomena (*Webster's New Twentieth Century Dictionary of the English Language*, unabridged, second edition [New York: Simon and Schuster, 1983], 37).

[11] Thomas Henry Huxley, *Lay Sermons, Addresses, and Reviews* (London: MacMillan and Co., 1870), chap. II "Emancipation—Black and White," emphasis added, online at http://www.gutenberg.org/files/16729/16729—8.txt (accessed March 10, 2006).

[12] It is a pervasive and consistent theme throughout Scripture that all people everywhere are created in the image of God and are of equal value (Genesis 1:27, 28; 9:6; James 3:9; cf. Ephesians 4:24; Colossians 3:10). "From one man [Adam] he made every nation of men, that they should inhabit the whole earth; and he determined the times set for them and the exact places where they should live" (Acts 17:26).

[13] Arthur Keith, *Evolution and Ethics* (New York: Putnam, 1947), 230. Also <http://reactorcore.org/evolution-and-

ethics.html> 27 March 2006.

14 Jacques Barzun, *Darwin, Marx, Wagner: Critique of a Heritage*, second ed. (Garden City, New York: Doubleday Anchor Books, 1958), 8. Barzun writes, "It is a commonplace that Marx felt his own work to be the exact parallel of Darwin's. He even wished to dedicate a portion of *Das Kapital* to the author of *The Origin of Species*."

15 Daniel Goleman, "Lost Paper Shows Freud's Effort to Link Analysis and Evolution," *The New York Times*, February 10, 1987, C1. Goleman explains further, "The evolutionary idea that Freud relied on most heavily in the manuscript is the maxim that 'ontogeny recapitulates phylogeny,' that is, that the development of the individual repeats the evolution of the entire species."

16 William Lane Craig, *Reasonable Faith: Christian Truth and Apologetics* (Wheaton, Ill.: Crossway Books, 1994), 59.

17 Craig, *Reasonable Faith*, 59.

18 Albert Camus, Stuart Gilbert, trans., *The Stranger* (New York. Vintage Books, 1942), 154.

19 James W. Sire, *The Universe Next Door*, 3rd ed. (Downers Grove, Ill.: IVP, 1997), 72.

20 Craig, *Reasonable Faith*, 60.

21 Craig, *Reasonable Faith*, 61.

22 *The Wonders of God's Creation: Planet Earth*, vol. 1, videotape (Chicago: Moody Institute of Science, 1993).

23 *The Wonders of God's Creation: Planet Earth*.

24 *The Wonders of God's Creation: Planet Earth*.

25 Guillermo Gonzalez and Jay W. Richards, *The Privileged Planet: How Our Place in the Cosmos is Designed for Discovery* (Washington D.C.: Regnery Publishing, 2004). I especially recommend the DVD based on this book: *The Privileged Planet: The Search for Purpose in the Universe* (La Habra, Calif.: Illustra Media, 2004), video.

Chapter Two: Resurrection

26 Dan Brown, *The Da Vinci Code* (New York: Doubleday, 2003).

27 For a point—by—point refutation of the claims made in *The Da Vinci Code* and a positive defense of the truth of Christianity, see Hank Hanegraaff and Paul L. Maier, *The Da Vinci Code: Fact or Fiction* (Wheaton, IL: Tyndale House Publishers, 2004).

28 Jeff Ayers, *Library Journal*, (February 1, 2003): 114.

29 *Publishers Weekly*, (March 18, 2003): 76.

30 Dan Brown, interview by Charles Gibson, *Good Morning America*, ABC, November 3, 2003. The material in this paragraph has been adapted from Hank Hanegraaff and Paul L. Maier, *The Da Vinci Code: Fact or Fiction* (Wheaton, IL: Tyndale House Publishers, 2004), vii–viii.

31 For a thorough refutation of each of these resurrection myths, see Hank Hanegraaff, *Resurrection* (Nashville: Word Publishing, 2000).

32 See Gary R. Habermas, *The Historical Jesus: Ancient Evidence for the Life of Christ* (Joplin, Mo.: College Press Publishing Co.,1996), 143–70 (see esp. 158); and William Lane Craig's argumentation in Paul Copan, ed., *Will the Real Jesus Please Stand Up? A Debate between William Lane Craig and John Dominic Crossan* (Grand Rapids: Baker Book House, 1998), 26–27.

33 The following medical data and descriptions concerning Christ's suffering adapted from C. Truman Davis, "The Crucifixion of Jesus: The Passion of Christ from a Medical Point of View," *Arizona Medicine* (March 1965): 183–87; and William D. Edwards, Wesley J. Gabel, and Floyd E. Hosmer, "On the Physical Death of Jesus Christ," The Journal of the *American Medical Association* (21 March 1986): 1455–63.

34 More specifically, the spikes were driven through Christ's wrists, which in Jewish understanding were part of the hands.

35 See Habermas, *The Historical Jesus*, 72–75.

36 See Richard N. Ostling, "Jesus Christ, Plain and Simple," *Time*, January 10, 1994, archived online at www.time.com.

37 John A.T Robinson, *The Human Face of God* (Philadelphia: Westminster, 1973), 131, as quoted by William Lane Craig in Copan, *Will the Real Jesus Please Stand Up?* 27.

38 Asserted by William Lane Craig in Copan, *Will the Real Jesus Please Stand Up?* 27.

39 See William Lane Craig, "Did Jesus Rise from the Dead?" in Michael J. Wilkins and J. P. Moreland, eds., *Jesus Under Fire: Modern Scholarship Reinvents the Historical Jesus* (Grand Rapids: Zondervan, 1995), 146–9; see also William Lane Craig, "Contemporary Scholarship and the Historical Evidence for the Resurrection of Jesus

Christ," *Truth 1* (1985): 89–95, from the Leadership University Web site at http://www.leaderu.com/truth/
1truth22.html (accessed March 10, 2006).

40 Lee Strobel, *The Case for Christ: A Journalist's Personal Investigation of the Evidence for Jesus* (Grand Rapids:
ZondervanPublishingHouse, 1998), 217, 218.

41 Paragraph adapted from William Lane Craig, "Did Jesus Rise from the Dead?" in Michael J. Wilkins and J. P.
Moreland, eds., *Jesus Under Fire: Modern Scholarship Reinvents the Historical Jesus* (Grand Rapids:
Zondervan, 1995), 152.

42 William Lane Craig, "Did Jesus Rise from the Dead?" in Michael J. Wilkins and J. P. Moreland, eds., *Jesus Under Fire:
Modern Scholarship Reinvents the Historical Jesus* (Grand Rapids: Zondervan, 1995), 147, 153; William Lane
Craig, *Reasonable Faith: Christian Truth and Apologetics* (Wheaton, Ill.: Crossway Books, 1994), 273.

43 Gary R. Habermas, *The Historical Jesus: Ancient Evidence for the Life of Christ* (Joplin, Mo.: College Press
Publishing Co., 1996), 154; cf. Craig L. Blomberg, "Where Do We Start Studying Jesus?" in Wilkins and
Moreland, *Jesus Under Fire*, 42–43.

44 On the rate at which legend accumulates, see Craig, *Reasonable Faith*, 284–85.

45 Paul received this creed from the believing community (1 Corinthians 15:3), perhaps from Peter and James in
Jerusalem in A.D. 36 (see Galatians 1:18–19), if not sooner (see Habermas, The Historical Jesus, 155; Craig,
Reasonable Faith, 273).

46 C. H. Dodd, "The Appearances of the Risen Christ: A Study in the Form Criticism of the Gospels," in *More New
Testament Studies* (Manchester: University of Manchester, 1968), 128, as quoted in William Lane Craig,
Reasonable Faith: Christian Truth and Apologetics (Wheaton, Ill.: Crossway Books, 1994), 282.

47 Craig, *Reasonable Faith*, 282.

48 Norman Perrin, *The Resurrection according to Matthew, Mark, and Luke* (Philadelphia: Fortress, 1977), 80, as
quoted by William Lane Craig in Paul Copan, ed., *Will the Real Jesus Please Stand Up? A Debate between
William Lane Craig and John Dominic Crossan* (Grand Rapids: Baker Books, 1998), 28.

49 Simon Greenleaf, *The Testimony of the Evangelists: The Gospels Examined by the Rules of Evidence* (Grand
Rapids: Kregel Classics, 1995; originally published 1874), 31–32.

50 See 1 Corinthians 15:5, in which the original apostles, minus Judas, are referred to as the Twelve (cf. John 20:24).

51 See Clement of Rome (c. A.D. 30–100), *First Epistle to the Corinthians*, chap. V; Tertullian (c. 160–225), *On
Prescription Against Heretics*, chap. XXXVI; Eusebius (c. 260–340), *History of the Church*, Book II:XXV.

52 See Eusebius, *History of the Church*, Book. III:I, where Eusebius quotes Origen (c. A.D. 185–254) concerning Peter's crucifixion.

53 Kenneth Barker, gen. ed., *The NIV Study Bible* (Grand Rapids: Zondervan, 1985), 1879.

54 Eusebius, Bk. II: XXIII. Cf. Josephus, *Antiquities*, 20:9:1; see John P. Meier, *A Marginal Jew: Rethinking the Historical
Jesus*, vol. 1 (New York: Doubleday, 1991), 57–59.

Chapter Three: Origin of the Bible

55 Theodore Roosevelt did not use the Bible in his inaugural oath in 1901.

56 Showtime, *Penn and Teller: Bull S#*!*, "Bible: Fact or Fiction," Thursday July 22, 2004.

57 John Shelby Spong, *Rescuing the Bible from Fundamentalism* (HarperSanFrancisco, 1991), 225, see 15–24, 212.

58 Spong, *Rescuing the Bible*, 21.

59 Spong, *Rescuing the Bible*, passim.

60 The New Testament was originally written in Greek. Nearly all of these extant Greek manuscripts predate the
invention of the printing press, and some 800 predate A.D. 1000. Lee Strobel, interviewing Dr. Bruce Metzger
of Princeton Theological Seminary, writes:

"'While papyrus manuscripts represent the earliest copies of the New Testament, there are also ancient
copies written on parchment, which was made from the skins of cattle, sheep, goats and antelope.
'We have what are called uncial manuscripts, which are written in all–capital Greek letters,' Metzger
explained. 'Today we have 306 of these, several dating back as early as the third century. The most important
are *Codex Sinaiticus*, which is the only complete New Testament in uncial letters, and *Codex Vaticanus*, which
is not quite complete. Both date to about A.D. 350.

'A new style of writing, more cursive in nature, emerged in roughly A.D. 800. It's called minuscule, and we
have 2, 856 of these manuscripts. Then there are also lectionaries, which contain New Testament Scripture in

the sequence it was to be read in the early churches at appropriate times during the year. A total of 2,403 of these have been cataloged. That puts the grand total of Greek manuscripts at 5,664.'" (Lee Strobel, *The Case for Christ* (Grand Rapids: Zondervan, 1998, 62–63).

The acronym L–U–M–P can be used as a memory aid so as not to *lump* all manuscripts together—Lexionaries, Uncials, Miniscules, and Papyri.

61 See Carsten Peter Thiede and Matthew d'Ancona, *Eyewitness to Jesus* (New York: Doubleday, 1996), 29–31, chap. 5; Philip Wesley Comfort, "Texts and Manuscripts of the New Testament," in Philip Wesley Comfort, ed. *The Origin of the Bible* (Wheaton: Tyndale House Publishers, 1992), 179–207; cf. Paul Barnett, *Is the New Testament Reliable?* (Downers Grove, Ill.: InterVarsity Press, 1986), 33–48. The earliest New Testament manuscript fragments date to the first and second centuries A.D., within 30–50 years of the original writing. More than 40 extant Greek manuscripts date *before* the fourth century—several from the second century—collectively composing most of the New Testament. The earliest extant copy of an entire New Testament text is *Codex Sinaiticus* (c. 350); *Codex Vaticanus* (c. 325) also contains the entire New Testament except Pastoral Epistles and Revelation. Note also that virtually the entire New Testament can be reconstructed from quotations found in the writings of the early church fathers.

According to New Testament scholar Craig Blomberg, the standard dating of the Gospels, for example, accepted even among very liberal scholars sets "Mark in the 70's, Matthew and Luke in the 80's, and John in the 90's." If so, Blomberg points out, even these dates are well within the lifetimes of the "eyewitnesses of the life of Jesus, including hostile eyewitnesses who would have served as a corrective if false teachings about Jesus were going around" (Lee Strobel, *The Case for Christ* [Grand Rapids: Zondervan, 1998], 33). Of course, if the earliest extant manuscripts do indeed date to the first century, then the original writing of the New Testament would be pushed back even earlier, and *a fortiori* the New Testament was written within the lifetimes of the community that bore witness to the events described therein.

62 F.F. Bruce, *The New Testament Documents: Are They Reliable?* (Downers Grove, Ill.: InterVarsity Press, 1960, reprinted 1978), 16; Bruce M. Metzger, *The Text of the New Testament: Its Transmission, Corruption, and Restoration*, 3rd ed. (New York: Oxford University Press, 1992), 34.

63 For further study, see Walter C. Kaiser, Jr., *The Old Testament Documents: Are They Reliable and Relevant?* (Downers Grove: Ill.: 2001).

64 For further study, see Paul L. Maier, *In the Fullness of Time: A Historian Looks at Christmas, Easter, and the Early Church* (HarperSanFrancisco, 1991).

65 See William M Ramsay, *The Bearing of Recent Discovery on the Trustworthiness of the New Testament*, reprint ed. (Grand Rapids, MI: Baker, 1953).

66 Jeffrey L. Sheler, "Is the Bible True?" *U. S. News and World Report*, 25 October 1999, 58; reprinted from Jeffrey L. Sheler, *Is the Bible True?* (San Francisco: HarperSanFrancisco, 1999).

67 See Sheler, *Is the Bible True?* 58–59.

68 See also Paul L. Maier, *In the Fullness of Time: A Historian Looks at Christmas, Easter, and the Early Church* (HarperSanFrancisco, 1991), 145 ff.

69 Sheler, *Is the Bible True?* 59. Sheler discusses other archaeological and historical insights of recent years, including the House of David inscription at Dan, which affirms the historicity of King David (54–58).

70 Nelson Glueck, *Rivers in the Desert* (New York: Farrar, Straus, and Cudahy, 1968), 31; as quoted in Henry M. Morris, *That Their Words May Be Used Against Them* (San Diego: Institute for Creation Research, 1997), 231.

71 For further study on the astounding archaeological support for the Bible, see Paul L. Maier, "Archaeology: Biblical Ally or Adversary?" *Christian Research Journal*, Vol. 27 /No. 2 (2004), available online at www.equip.org.

72 Chapters 2 and 7 of the Old Testament book of Daniel describe Daniel's prophecies related to the coming kingdom; Daniel's vision in chapter 8 represents details of Antiochus Epiphanes' reign in the second century BC. The "horn" that "started small but grew in power…until it reached the host of the heavens" represents Antiochus Epiphanes.

Chapter Seven: Eternal Perspective
73 C.S. Lewis, *Mere Christianity* (New York: Collier Books, 1952), 104, emphasis added.
74 Dallas Willard, *The Divine Conspiracy: Rediscovering our Hidden Life in God* (HarperSanFrancisco, 1998), 213.
75 Dallas Willard, *The Divine Conspiracy*, 208.

FOR MORE INFORMATION

Promise Keepers

www.promisekeepers.com

Promise Keepers is dedicated to igniting and uniting men to be passionate followers of Jesus Christ through the effective communication of the 7 Promises. Promise Keepers seeks to unite Christian men of all races, denominations, ages, cultures, and socio-economic groups, and believes that men need accountable relationships with other men. Those relationships—along with prayer, Bible study, and active church membership—help men in their daily life with God, their families, and their communities.

Thomas S. Fortson, Jr.

Thomas S. Fortson is President and CEO of Promise Keepers. Before joining the Promise Keepers staff in 1996, Dr. Fortson spent many years in corporate America and has an abundance of experience in ministry organizations. In addition, he and his wife, Toni, have been speakers for more than fifteen years with Campus Crusade for Christ's ministry to married couples. The Fortsons reside in the Denver, Colorado, area and have three adult children.

Hank Hanegraaff

www.equip.org

Hank Hanegraaff serves as president and chairman of the board of the North Carolina-based Christian Research Institute International (CRI). He also hosts CRI's *Bible Answer Man* program, which is broadcast daily across the United States and Canada. He is the author of popular books, including *The Bible Answer Book*, *Resurrection, The Prayer of Jesus,* and *Fatal Flaws.* In additionn, he is the co-author of *The Da Vinci Code: Fact or Fiction?* and The Last Disciple fiction series. Hank and his wife, Kathy, live in North Carolina and are the parents of nine children.